I Am Dr. SEONGLIM JIN, a Pulmonologist

"Dreaming of hopes for patients with a tight chest who are breathless"

I Am Dr. SEONGLIM JIN, a Pulmonologist
Dreaming of hopes for patients with a tight chest who are breathless

First printing edition November 24th, 2024

Author SEONGLIM JIN
Publisher GILSOO JANG
Publishing House Knowledge and Sensitivity#
Publication Registration Number 2012-000081

Editing & Proofreader Knowledge and Sensitivity#
Marketing YUNGIL KIM, EUNHYE JUNG

Address 1212, 50-3 Dearung 6. Gasan-dong, Geumcheon-gu, Seoul
Phone 070-4651-3730 to 4
Fax 070-4325-7006
Email ksbookup@naver.com
Website www.knsbookup.com

ISBN 979-11-392-2228-9(03810)
price 25,000won

Please approach seller for the exchange of books with printing errors.
The use of all or part of this book and its contents will require prior permission from the copyright holder and the publisher.

Knowledge and Sensitivity#
Go to homepage

I Am Dr. SEONGLIM JIN, a Pulmonologist

"Dreaming of hopes for patients with a tight chest who are breathless"

Written by
Director of the Beautiful Breath Clinic Dr. **SEONGLIM JIN**

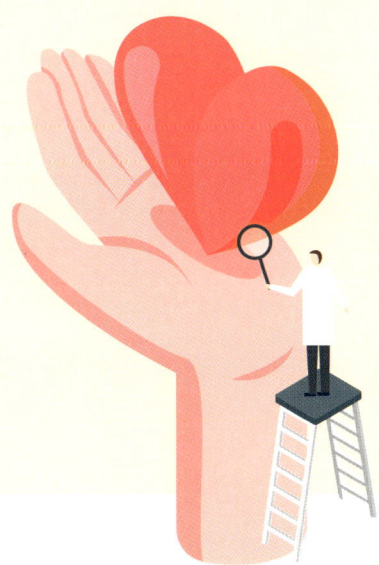

The Story of Those who Are out of Breath with Tight Chests.

A story of a pulmonologist that begins with the hope that South Korea's essential healthcare policy will go in the right direction.

knowledge & sensibility

〚 Foreword 〛

Respiratory disease is one of the biggest blind spots in medical journalism.

This is because many intractable diseases cannot be cured with a single surgery or medication. Consequently, unsubstantiated treatments are often hyped commercially and marketed to patients as special prescriptions. This is where pulmonologist Dr. SEONGLIM JIN stands out. He started the Beautiful Breath Clinic, which is the first specialty clinic in the community to offer state-of-the-art treatment for various respiratory diseases.

This place definitely has the skills and equipment to obviate the need to go to a high-profile university hospital. The doctor is also passionate about patient education. His livestreaming on the YouTube channel "@aftertherainkr" is popular among subscribers, as they can see his genuine concern for his patients. It is such a treat to be able to read his stories in a book now. May his wisdom and knowledge be of great benefit to many patients who struggle with shortness of breath.

Hong Hye-geol, M.D.,
creator of South Korea's first medical YouTube channel "@aftertherainkr"

〚 Prologue 〛

Human life begins with one's first breath. The first cry of a newborn heralds a dynamic and emotional moment, announcing their presence in the world.

Once a human life begins, its end is marked with the "last breath." Breathing is an act that accompanies us from the moment we are born to the moment we die.

I am a pulmonologist.

What does a pulmonologist do? Pulmonologists play a pivotal role in one of the most talked-about "essential healthcare" topics in the country these days.

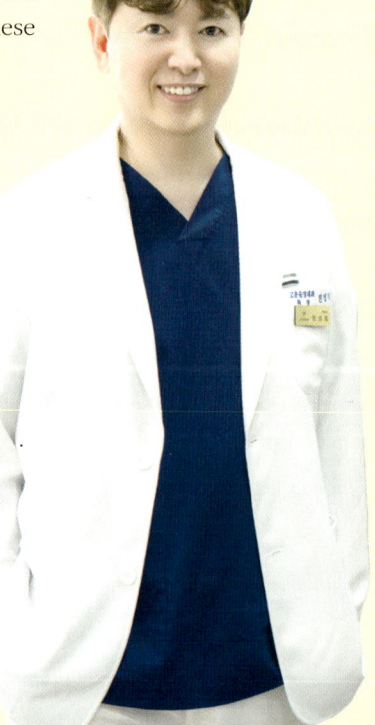

Dr. SEONGLIM JIN,
Director of the Beautiful Breath Clinic

They accurately identify the causes of various respiratory diseases that humans experience and provide appropriate treatment according to their diagnosis. As a specialist in respiratory medicine, dealing with potentially life-threatening conditions is an "essential" medical discipline.

The global COVID-19 pandemic brought respiratory medicine into the public eye. The COVID-19 pandemic, which began in December 2019, was a major event in 2020 that not only caused a severe health crisis in our country and worldwide but also had a major impact on countries' finances and individuals' economic lives. As doctors and nurses in protective suits treated patients with COVID-19, people witnessed firsthand how life-threatening a tiny, invisible virus could be.

Knowing that the dreaded COVID-19 can be contracted through the respiratory tract and spread in the form of droplets (i.e., secretions released when an infected person sneezes), it has come to the public's attention that a medical specialty called "respiratory medicine" exists.

Pulmonologists see more critically ill patients than many other specialists in internal medicine, frequently treat emergency patients in critical condition, and care for their patients with great sensitivity, all the while exposing themselves to infectious diseases such as tuberculosis, pneumonia, flu, and COVID-19. Thus, the work itself is demanding, difficult, dangerous, and stressful.

In this age of work-life balance, given the difficult, demanding, high-risk, and low-reward nature of the specialty of pulmonary medicine, the decline in the number of doctors who choose to become pulmonologists is unsurprising. This makes sense considering human instinct.

Pulmonologists, as the doctors who treat human breathing problems, often experience parting from their patients. Parting with a loved one is not merely difficult; it is incredibly difficult. Parting in a relationship is hard because it indicates loss.

Feelings of excitement and comfort calm people and remind them that they matter. While it may vary for different people, parting with a loved one does not happen frequently in life. However, pulmonologists must frequently part with patients. In this job, one is bound to experience frequent loss. A sense of loss is a manifestation of emptiness, hollowness, and loneliness. After 30 years as a physician, I am still not immune to the whirlwind of emotions. Over time, I have met a lot of patients with severe respiratory disease, leading me to develop a new belief: just one more thought before losing hope.

The saying "the boughs that bear the most fruit hang the lowest" is one I always keep in mind when diagnosing and treating difficult patients. Making it through each day with the humility to think and do just one more thing, even for the most difficult patient, can add up and become my life and my patient's happiness.

Aside from under unusual circumstances, human nature is likely to favor things that are easy, safe, and well-rewarded. Rewards do not necessarily mean financial rewards, as without them people are often happy with their behavior and choices, as long as they feel sufficiently rewarded elsewhere.

This book does not aim to discuss the collapse of essential healthcare. The word "essential" means "necessary or required." Thus, essential healthcare includes healthcare services that must be available or should be provided. In fact, the very idea that essential healthcare could become a social problem is nonsense. What I would like to do with this book is narrate the story of "patients who are out of breath with a tight chest."

Through the inexpressible suffering of patients with various serious respiratory diseases and their families, I would like to reflect on the suffering caused by the "challenges of human existence" and consider how those of us who live in this era can help patients with respiratory diseases by understanding their struggles. This is the story of a pulmonologist who desperately hopes that the distorted and twisted essential healthcare policy of South Korea will develop in the right direction, through the small cries of a physician with 30 years of experience who has met more than two million patients with respiratory diseases and deeply empathizes with their suffering.

"May this moment of today be your day."

March 16, 2024, looking at the healthcare crisis.

Dr. SEONGLIM JIN,
Director of the Beautiful Breath Clinic, a Pulmonologist

With proud colleagues at the Beautiful Breath Clinic.

〚 Table of Contents 〛

Foreword • 5
Prologue • 6

Chapter 1
01 The secrets of the disease of despondency • 14
02 CPR, the unavoidable destiny of essential healthcare doctors • 27
03 Why Anam-dong? • 34
04 Can you enjoy your life? • 41
05 Fate determined in a "split second" • 47
06 One word to live by • 54

Chapter 2
01 Unimaginable pain of shortness of breath • 62
02 Characteristics of fatal pneumonia and pneumonia in older adults • 71
03 Is Seoul National University Hospital the best option? • 76
04 Sincerity is the way of Heaven • 83
05 Diagnoses lie in the words of patients • 88

Chapter 3
01 Watch out for kind doctors • 96
02 A country where helping a poor patient is a crime • 101
03 On the importance of discernment • 108
04 The quintessential preaching to deaf ears • 115
05 The paradox of prognosis • 123
06 The truth and lies of HIRA healthcare quality assessment • 129

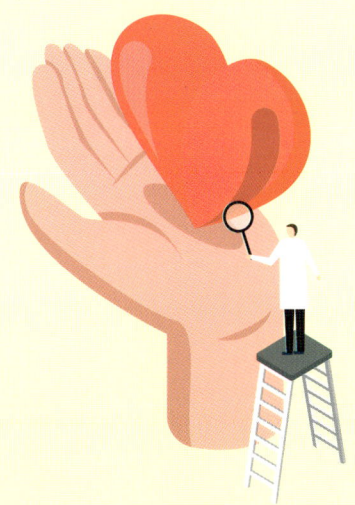

Chapter 4	01 Mind your Ps and Qs • 138
	02 No good deed goes unpunished • 143
	03 Uninvited Guests • 147
	04 Drug Utilization Review(DUR) • 152
	05 Reality and illusion of symptoms • 160

Chapter 5	01 Emotional outlet • 170
	02 Memory lane • 175
	03 Namhansanseong Fortress • 180
	04 Exit strategy • 185
	05 Try to go south by driving the chariot north • 190
	06 Perspectives onlife and death • 197

Chapter 6	One last thing to say to patients before closing the book: a good doctor is a doctor who has just one more thought • 204

Epilogue • 211

Chapter 1

The secrets of the disease of despondency

―

CPR, the unavoidable destiny of essential healthcare doctors

―

Why Anam-dong?

―

Can you enjoy your life?

―

Fate determined in a "split second"

―

One word to live by

01
The secrets of the disease of despondency

In my life, the rivers and mountains have changed five times. Soon, I will witness their sixth change. When someone has already lived more days than they have left, it may imply that they have been through the storms of life.

This book is a reflection of my experiences and life as a physician. It is a collection of stories ranging from the distant past of my days in medical school to my near-present experiences in 2024. As a physician who has been treating patients for 30 years, constituting nearly half of my life, the most frustrating thing I see is despondency in patients. Patients do not develop such despondency on their own; doctors teach them to live with it.

Doctors are the people who treat patients. Then why would physicians declare there is nothing more they can do for their patients, making them give up on themselves?

Remarkable advances have been made in the field of medicine. What kind of disease is this that doctors are telling patients to quit? Even patients with stage IV lung cancer can be treated without giving up. The term end-stage lung cancer is not used, as it implies a sense of defeat and that there is no cure.

When I opened my practice 23 years ago, if I diagnosed patients with bronchial asthma, they gave up on treatment out of the belief that it was incurable. Such a misconception is not of the patients' own making. Doctors had told those patients that bronchial asthma was an "incurable" disease, as they did not know enough about it.

The pathogenesis of bronchial asthma was not fully elucidated until the early 1990s. Until 1980, bronchial asthma was considered to be caused by the contraction of bronchial smooth muscle. Since the cause of the disease was known to be bronchoconstriction, it was treated with medication to open up the narrowed bronchi.

Medical advances come with advancements in science. Advances in natural science have led to advances in pathology, the study of how diseases work. Pathology refers to the identification of the exact cause of a disease. Advances in treatment do not simply occur on their own. Medical treatment evolves through repeated pioneering attempts by wise physicians and the accumulation of their results.

Bronchial asthma involves the narrowing of the bronchial tubes. Bronchial asthma is exacerbated by exposure to external allergens or by dust, pollution, viruses, and bacteria invading one's airways. Is that not the obvious conclusion?

The lining of the bronchi becomes inflamed and narrowed, causing the patient to feel short of breath, cough, and wheeze, making a whistling sound.

There are always pioneers in life. A pioneer is someone who realizes something before the public does. Pioneers are often mocked and ostracized initially. They propose new principles that completely overturn existing conventions and advocate for changes in treatment. They challenge the comfort and familiarity of the medical world. They were certainly reckless in their endeavors, and conservative doctors would have probably criticized the leading doctors for such attempts.

That was a time when bronchial asthma was treated with a fast-acting oral bronchodilator called "Ventolin," which stabilized the patient and relaxed the bronchial smooth muscle.

Leading doctors wondered why the smooth muscle of the bronchi would contract in the presence of bronchial asthma. Doctors needed to adopt a mindset of constantly questioning the disease. Finally, the leading doctors made up their minds.

About what?

They decided to perform a "bronchoscopy" on patients with bronchial asthma.

Readers may wonder what this means. Here is an easy example for explanation. In bronchial asthma, the mucous membrane lining the bronchi becomes inflamed, and requires as urgent a response as it would if it were "on fire." Under this condition, the doctor attempts to take tissue from the inflamed bronchial mucosa through bronchoscopy.

If a mucous membrane is on fire, the surrounding mucous membranes will be destroyed. The idea of taking a piece of devastated bronchial mucosa from an asthmatic patient sounds too dangerous and bizarre to me even today. However, leading doctors have done it.

Such attempts have changed the definition of bronchial asthma. For years, bronchial asthma was believed to be caused by the constriction of bronchial tubes. However, it has since been scientifically proven that bronchoconstriction is caused by chronic inflammation of the bronchial mucosa.

Now, the underlying cause of bronchial asthma is known. Given the cause, all there is left is to address it. Learning that the underlying cause is chronic inflammation of the bronchi led to a change in treatment.

Conventional treatment included medication to dilate constricted bronchial tubes. As the underlying cause was chronic inflammation, treating bronchial asthma with dilators without anti-inflammatory effects did not improve the condition. Therefore, doctors felt comfortable telling patients that it was an "incurable" disease.

How do patients feel if they are diagnosed with an incurable disease? Some patients may give up on treatment, while others may fight tooth and nail to make it through. The important thing is that the moment the doctors have declared a disease as incurable, they no longer have to deal with the complaints of the patients. The declaration of an incurable disease sets the doctors free, while the patients have to endure not only the hardships and emotional pain of life but also the risk of serious complications and loss of life from giving up on treating their asthma.

In 2024, no doctor in South Korea would call bronchial asthma an "incurable" disease. The same is true for patients. Bronchial asthma is a disease that is controlled by treating inflammation, for which steroid medications are essential. Oral steroid medications are used for severe or steroid-dependent asthma.
However, oral steroid medications are often associated with many adverse events. Therefore, inhaled steroids, with very few systemic adverse events, are the key treatment for bronchial asthma.

With the advent of inhaled steroids and bronchodilators, bronchial asthma has become manageable rather than incurable.
Bronchial asthma is one of the various respiratory diseases that has shed the stigma of the disease of despondency. After 40 years, bronchial asthma is now recognized as a manageable condition.
Readers should note one thing here. I have not said that bronchial asthma is a curable condition. It is not curable, but it is manageable. The same is true for hypertension and diabetes. Hypertension is controlled by taking blood pressure medication; however, this does not mean that one can stop taking blood pressure medication after a few months.
The concept of cure is defined as the absence of relapse without the need for medication. For example, patients who develop appendicitis and have their appendix surgically removed are considered cured. The anatomical organ called the appendix is removed; thus, they will never experience appendicitis again.
This is the idea of a cure. Bronchial asthma flares up. It recurs when exposed to allergens, viruses, or cold air. This means that it is not curable but manageable. With good management, medications can be reduced or even discontinued. Other respiratory diseases have carried

the stigma of being incurable for almost as long as asthma, but remain that way today, such as bronchiectasis.

Some doctors continue to inform patients that nothing can be done for bronchiectasis and that they should just live with it. These doctors must have never diagnosed, treated, or given any deep consideration to bronchiectasis.

Such statements are casually made even by doctors in pulmonology departments at university hospitals. Giving such an explanation to a patient with bronchiectasis shatters their will and destroys any hope they may have, even in pulmonology departments. This leaves patients in a state of despondency.

What is bronchiectasis? Why is it still considered an incurable disease, thus leading patients to forgo treatment and doctors to avoid treating it?

Bronchiectasis is a condition in which the bronchi are permanently stretched owing to abnormalities in the muscles of the bronchial wall and loss of elasticity.

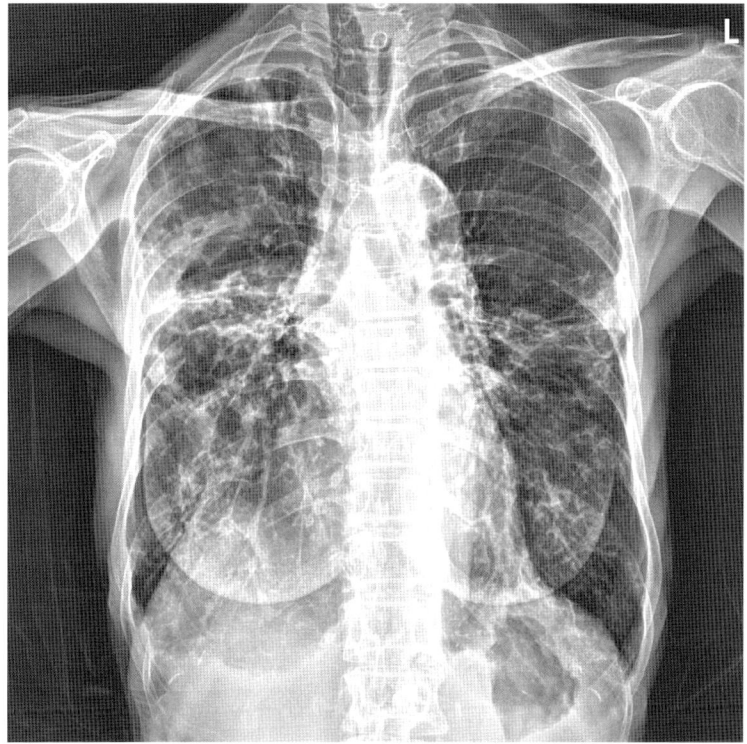

Simple chest radiograph of a patient with bronchiectasis:
white areas in both lungs.

Bronchiectasis is characterized by severe sputum. This is not just any sputum; it is yellow, sticky, and, in severe cases, thick enough to block the bronchial tubes, causing difficulty breathing.

The symptom that patients fear the most with bronchiectasis is hemoptysis, the appearance of blood in the sputum. Massive hemoptysis is a serious condition that can be fatal if not treated immediately.

In addition to these typical clinical symptoms, other symptoms may include chest tightness and pain and generalized weakness. If bronchiectasis is not treated promptly, complications can develop, including pneumonia and bronchial pneumonia, which are inflammation of the lungs; empyema, a pus-filled sac in the pleura that surrounds the lungs; pneumothorax, a tear in the pleura; brain abscess, a pus-filled sac in the brain; and pulmonary tuberculosis.

Patients are particularly vulnerable to nontuberculous mycobacteria, an atypical form of tuberculosis. Every disease has a cause. While modern medicine does not know the causes of all diseases, bronchiectasis is most often caused as a sequela of childhood pertussis, measles, respiratory viruses, bacterial infections, and tuberculosis.
The root cause of bronchiectasis is infection, for which the main treatment is antibiotic therapy. The two main principles of bronchiectasis treatment are effective airway clearance and sputum management, whereas the other important principle is appropriate antibiotic treatment.

As there are many misconceptions about antibiotic treatment and many different types of antibiotics, seeking professional help is important for antibiotic treatment. Antibiotic treatment is typically empirical, and doctors choose antibiotics according to their experience. However, when treating bronchiectasis or pneumonia, accurate and rapid treatment requires identifying the causative bacteria and testing for antibiotic resistance to determine the antibiotics to which patients will respond positively.

Other treatments aside from these two standard ones commonly used to manage bronchiectasis include active cycle of breathing techniques, respiratory control such as chest expansion exercises, forced expiratory breathing, and respiratory physiotherapy.

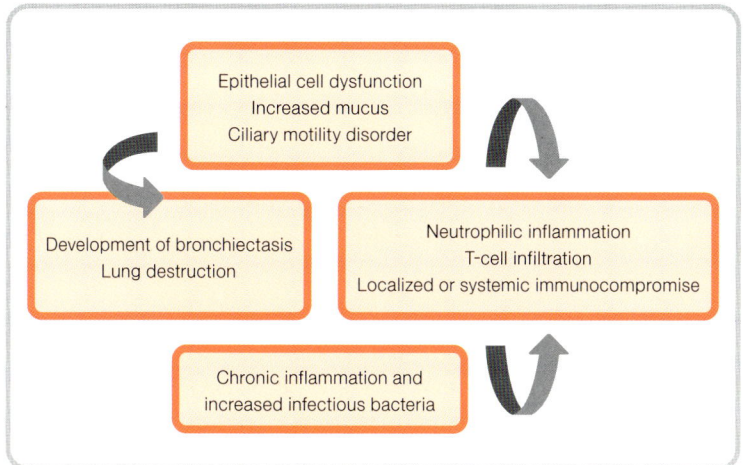

Pathogenesis of bronchiectasis.

These breathing techniques are not just helpful in treating bronchiectasis but could also help manage chronic obstructive pulmonary disease(COPD).
Bronchiectasis usually causes a lot of sputum to stick to the bronchial walls, which can be expelled by tapping the lower chest area with a cupped palm. In recent times, a "chest vibrator," which taps on the chest wall, has been used to help.

While most cases of bronchiectasis can be controlled using the methods described above, some severe cases may not respond to standard treatment.
In "severe bronchiectasis," the sputum not only adheres to the bronchial walls but is sufficiently sticky and abundant to completely block the bronchi. This situation can be likened to water being trapped in a reservoir and going stale and stagnant.
Sputum in the bronchi should be considered as a foreign object stuck in and obstructing the bronchi. No amount of antibiotic injections or oral antibiotics will resolve pus-like sputum blocking the bronchi.
It is like a lump of pus on an arm or leg that has been there for a long

time. It is not a condition that can be resolved medically with internal medicine but requires surgical resection to save the patient's life.

If an unresolved colony of bacteria forms a tumor-like mass that is not excised, the bacteria can enter the bloodstream and cause sepsis, a potentially life-threatening condition in which the entire body is attacked by bacteria. Treatment for severe bronchiectasis requires a bronchoscopic procedure to remove the pus-like, foreign body-like sputum blocking the bronchi.

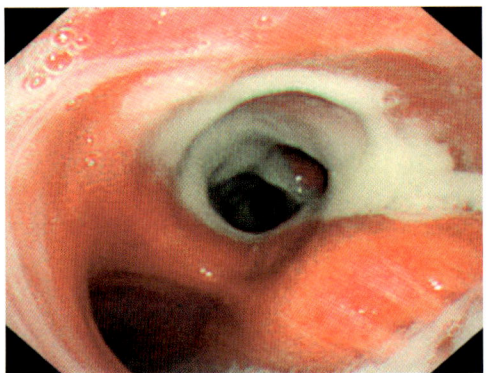

A bronchial view of a patient with bronchiectasis: filled with pus-like sputum.

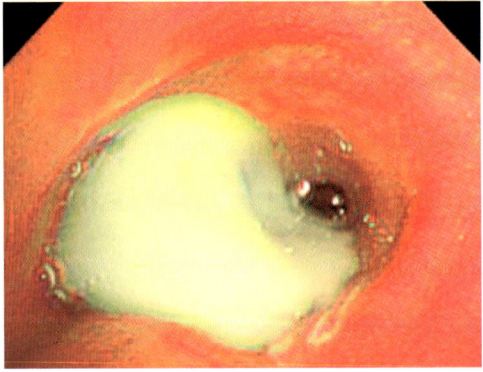

Bronchiectasis: purulent sputum completely blocking the airway.

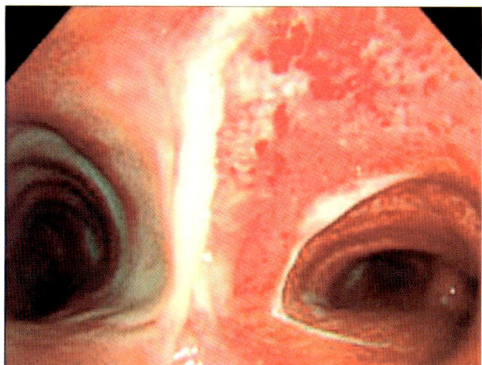

Bronchoscopy procedure to clear sputum from blocked airways.

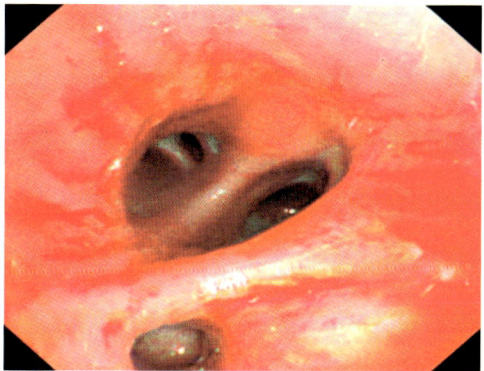

A view after bronchoscopy to clear sputum.

Removing a large clump of sputum is not the end of treatment, but the beginning.

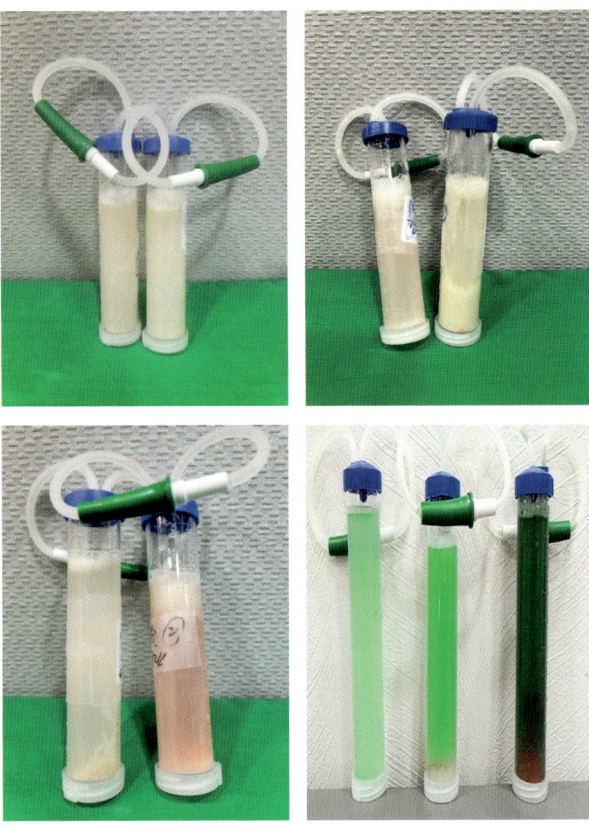

Bronchoscopy to clear bronchi and examine sputum
Light yellow/gray/dark yellow/red/light green/green sputum.

A good first step can make all the difference not only in healthcare but in many other areas of life as well.

However, a good start is also no guarantee that things will work out eventually. Nevertheless, there are many stories of those who started out as failures but persevered to overcome their initial struggles and achieve success.

When we watch a sports game, we get more excited when a team that was initially losing eventually wins, cheering that it was "a close game." Rooting for the weak over the strong, and feeling joy when the weak succeeds, is human nature. This is likely because life in the modern era is difficult on its own. Since our lives are weary and troublesome, do we not expect hope and long for an outcome beyond our expectations?

This scenario is common in many dramas. We often see dramatic resuscitations of dying patients and even incurable cases where a heroic doctor, against all odds, miraculously saves a patient from the brink of death. These situations are set up to provide the viewer with a dramatic stimulation. A real doctor should not expect miracles in a situation where the patient's condition is deteriorating.

What is the difference between a pro and an amateur? An amateur has only one response to a given situation, whereas a pro has multiple options.

A good doctor knows exactly what the patient's condition is, does not expect miracles, and can help the patient understand their condition and anticipate their quality of life after treatment and what they will face again. It is important to realize that bronchiectasis is not an incurable disease with no remedy.

Bronchiectasis is not an ailment that patients just have to live with until they die. What kind of doctor tells a patient with hypertension or diabetes that they have an incurable disease? Which patients fall into a state of despondency?

Bronchiectasis is a chronic disease that affects the airway. The term chronic means that lifelong treatment is required. Hypertension, diabetes, and COPD are chronic conditions that require appropriate management and treatment. Bronchiectasis is a progressive disease if left untreated. Therefore, seeking medical attention is crucial. The New England Journal of Medicine (NEJM), a top medical journal, published an article on seven reasons to treat bronchiectasis in its November 2022 issue.

Both doctors and patients should keep in mind that bronchiectasis is not a disease of despondency. It is a disease to be fought against and that can be overcome with a resilient spirit.

Seven Reasons to Treat Bronchiectasis

NEJM November, 2022

1) Destruction of bronchi and lungs
2) Shortening of life
3) Decreased quality of life
4) Risk for infection
5) Burden of economic risk
6) Burden on family and friends
7) National human and economic losses

02
CPR, the unavoidable destiny of essential healthcare doctors

March 9, 2024, at 8:30 am.

I was seeing patients as usual. To be more precise, I was performing a biopsy via bronchoscopy on a patient with suspected lung cancer.

Not all tumors in the lungs are malignant. However, the radiological findings of this patient's chest CT were suggestive of malignancy. Lung cancer can be broadly categorized into two types: small cell carcinoma with small cancer cells and non-small cell carcinoma with large cancer cells.

The classification of lung cancer is crucial, as the treatment regimens are completely different, and the prognosis varies greatly. Small cell carcinoma is not curable surgically, can be treated with chemotherapy, and has no targeted gene therapies. In contrast, non-small cell carcinoma can be treated surgically unless it is stage IV, and more than a dozen targeted therapies are available for adenocarcinoma in particular, depending on the type of gene expression.

Hence, when a bronchoscopy is performed to biopsy lung cancer, the pulmonologist who performs the procedure takes as many tissue samples as possible and sends them to a pathologist. This allows the pathologist to carefully and safely identify the exact nature of the lung cancer and help determine the best treatment for the patient.

The bronchoscopy room has the same tense atmosphere as the frontlines of a battlefield, with fully armed soldiers on guard duty, always at the highest alert. Just as I was wrapping up the examination, a staff member barged into the room. Before I even heard the staff member yell, I felt my hair stand on end. Cold sweat ran down my back, my heartbeat quickened, and my nerves were on edge.

I knew immediately that there was an emergency. I rushed out of the bronchoscopy room and headed for the waiting room, where there were a number of patients. I spotted a patient sitting in a wheelchair, gasping and asking for medical help. Having seen many emergency patients, I knew based on his appearance alone that this patient required immediate cardiopulmonary resuscitation (CPR). I immediately placed the patient on the floor of the waiting room, measured his oxygen saturation, and took his blood pressure.

While checking whether the patient was conscious, I called the 911 cardiac arrest call center with a "cardiac arrest emergency" report. In South Korea, the 911 dispatch system is so fast that the paramedics take only about four minutes, but for a cardiac arrest patient, those four minutes can determine life or death.

A procedure called the "CBA" must be performed on the patient within the first four minutes of cardiac arrest detection.

First, C, which stands for circulation, involves compressing the heart area to get blood from the heart to the brain. In CPR, compressions are the most important and must be performed immediately and correctly.

Second, B, which stands for breathing, involves checking the patient's breathing. While performing cardiac compressions, the patient's breathing is monitored. If the patient is not breathing, administer mouth-to-mouth resuscitation to blow air into their lungs. Specialists may be able to increase the chance of survival by intubating the patient orally and then pushing more fresh air into the lungs.

Third, A, which stands for airway management, involves maintaining the patient's airway to prevent the tongue or secretions in the mouth from blocking it.

This series of procedures occurs almost simultaneously. Even for the most competent doctor, the most important thing to do when seeing a patient in cardiac arrest is to call 911 immediately, and it is essential that the caller accurately states "cardiac arrest" and the location.

The way CPR is administered has changed from the days when I was in medical school. In the past, the order of "ABC" was emphasized instead of "CBA."

As a doctor, meeting a cardiac arrest patient is one of the most nerve-wracking moments, regardless of whether it happens inside or outside the hospital. The moment a doctor encounters a patient in cardiac arrest, their automatic reflexes should take over. As emergency CPR was initiated, the oxygen saturation of the patient increased from 0% to 70% and the asystolic heart began to pulse. I tried my best to keep the patient alive until the paramedics arrived, while the other patients in the waiting room witnessed it. Paramedics arrived and the patient was taken to the emergency room at the university hospital, thankfully alive.

Facing a CPR patient is an inevitable part of life as a doctor who makes a living providing essential healthcare. A doctor's job is to identify the cause of a disease, diagnose it, and treat it correctly. Cardiac arrest has two main causes.

CPR should be performed depending on the exact cause. The first thing to know is whether it is an asystole or a ventricular fibrillation-induced cardiac arrest.

For professional CPR, it is important to immediately get a defibrillator and check the heart rhythm. Whether the heart has stopped completely or is paralyzed should be determined. A completely ceased heart is asystole, whereas a paralyzed heart beats very rapidly and irregularly. After checking the heart rhythm of the patient with a defibrillator, if it is confirmed to be ventricular fibrillation, a 150-jolt defibrillation is performed, CPR is performed, epinephrine is injected, and the heart rhythm is checked again.

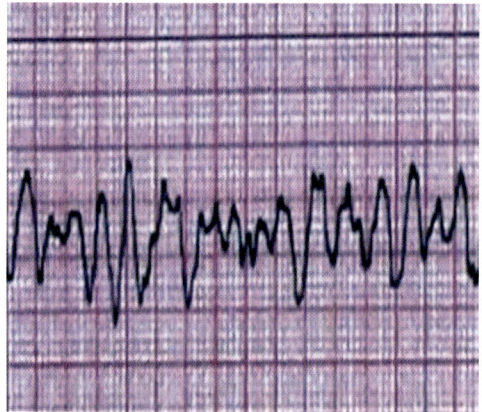

An electrocardiogram in ventricular fibrillation:
Use a defibrillator immediately.

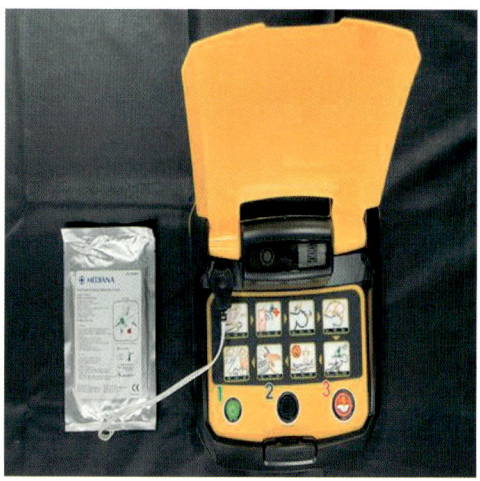

Photograph of the defibrillator at the Beautiful Breath Clinic.

If the heart does not return to rhythm and is asystolic, the patient should be intubated endotracheally. Endotracheal intubation is a procedure with a higher chance of success when performed by a pulmonologist or emergency physician.

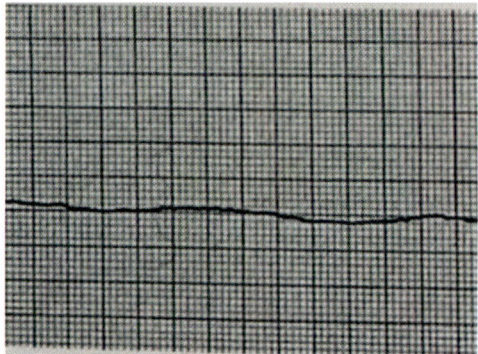

Asystole with no heartbeat, requiring endotracheal intubation.

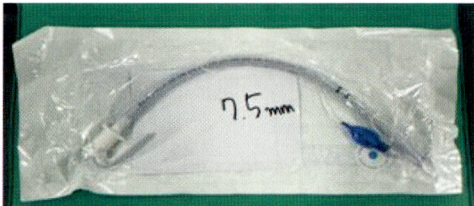

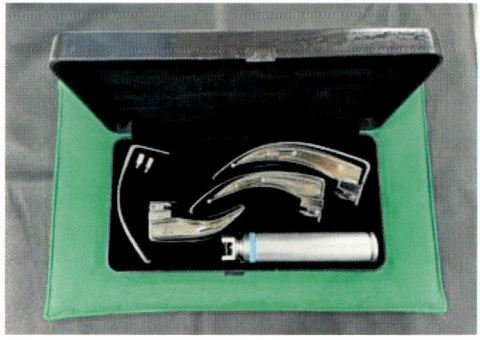

Intratracheal intubation devices readily available at the Beautiful Breath Clinic.

The Ministry of Health and Welfare announced recently that nurses will be allowed to perform endotracheal intubation in the course of their duties. This was in response to the healthcare crisis that began with the resignation of residents following the announcement to increase the number of medical school enrollments by 2,000. As someone who has performed CPR in real emergencies, this is a very unrealistic statement. This is not a matter of opinion, and it is a ridiculous guideline that can lead to the deaths of countless cardiac or respiratory emergency patients.

Intubation is not a simple procedure that can be performed easily. It is a procedure that should be carried out by a trained doctor or a first-class paramedic.

In any field, not just healthcare, listening to experts who have been there and know what they are talking about is important. Furthermore, when formulating policies that can have a profound impact on the lives of people now and in the future, it is important not to make decisions on the fly or for the sake of the moment. As healthcare is a highly specialized field, consultation with experts is essential.

Where are cardiac arrest patients most often found? At the hospital? On the street? No. The most common place to find a cardiac arrest patient is in their home. Therefore, CPR for cardiac arrest patients should be a national call to action for all adults.

When someone does something repeatedly for a long time and does it exceptionally well, we call them an "expert" or "master." In the medical world, such a person is referred to as the "best doctor."

There is a phenomenon called resistance, for which the dictionary provides three main definitions. First, resistance refers to the phenomenon in which the effectiveness of a drug is reduced by repeated use. A typical example of this is resistance to antibiotics because of misuse. Second, pathogens, such as bacteria, can develop resistance to chemotherapy treatments or continued use of antibiotics. Third, resistance can refer to an organism's ability to withstand changes in environmental conditions. (Source: Naver Dictionary)

As a pulmonologist, I have seen my fair share of emergencies, which should have helped me develop resistance in the general sense. Essential healthcare doctors are armed with resistance.

When I am treating an emergency patient, my sympathetic nerves are firing and my emotions are racing, with a million thoughts running through my head. I perform the procedure mechanically as I have been trained and instructed to do.

However, doctors are also human. The process of seeing and treating emergency patients is emotionally taxing and physically demanding. This is a special case in which no resistance is developed. I am now in my 30th year as a physician and have been a pulmonologist for 23 years. Even now, I become very nervous when I perform bronchoscopies, and I am under so much stress that my bones feel like they are melting when I am examining and treating critically ill patients.

The reason that essential healthcare is dying and doctors are abandoning it in favor of specialties such as dermatology, ophthalmology, and plastic surgery is not that they are shallow people chasing easy money. They choose their specialties to fulfill a natural human need, and the government, not doctors, is to blame for this bizarre healthcare structure.

The current healthcare crisis, which the government is pushing unilaterally under the guise of reforming essential healthcare, will evolve into a disaster and completely destroy the world's best healthcare system that South Korea's healthcare administration worked so hard to build.

South Korea's world-class healthcare system was built by exploiting the labor of residents in large hospitals. I worked over 140 hours a week during my resident days. What keeps residents going for those five long years is hope for the future.

Residents resign because their future dreams were stolen from them by an armchair theory. To restore our country's healthcare system, we must return to the residents their "dreams of the future."

This story comes at a crucial juncture in the ongoing healthcare disruption. By the time the book is published, I hope South Korea's advanced healthcare system will be thriving, with the government addressing the root causes of the shortage of essential healthcare providers to ensure better quality care for all.

03
Why Anam-dong?

During afternoon clinic hours on Thursday, March 7, 2024, a young woman presented with a sore throat and tightness in her chest. Young female patients make me nervous, which is not because I am a man.

Honestly, I get anxious when I see a young female patient, especially one in her early 20s. The wait times at our clinic are very long. It is not uncommon for patients to wait three hours, and on at least three of the five days a week that I work, the reception closes early in the morning. Young patients are rarely critically ill. Most of them have a cough as an aftereffect of a cold, reflux esophagitis, or gastritis. A few patients have bronchial asthma, bronchial tuberculosis, or pulmonary tuberculosis.

For patients with colds and sore throats, their time with the doctor often ends quickly. If a patient waits three hours and sees a doctor for only three minutes, they may be understandably upset. However, as a doctor, I do not have much to say.

Let me share a scene from when I see a patient with typical cold symptoms, with a sense of dryness like a documentary film, hoping that readers will understand.

"Hello? Please have a seat here." The patient sits in the chair in the office.

"You are Ms. Kim Soo-in(not the real name), right?"

"What brought you here?"

"I'm here with a cough and sore throat."

"How long have you been coughing? Do you have sputum? Have you had a fever recently?"

"Three days. No fever. No sputum."
"Let me do an auscultation. Please turn around."

After auscultating, I had already made a diagnosis. It was just a cold and a sore throat. No testing was required, and I prescribe cold medicine for three days.

I have been practicing medicine for 30 years. There is nothing more to ask or say to a patient with a simple cold. This is where the reactions of men and women show a marked difference. Men do not ask any questions or say anything else. A male patient in his 20s is silent.

A female patient in her 20s is completely different. She starts by saying what discomfort she has, and then moves on to several other things. A month ago, she watched a movie, drank coffee, and ate a burger with a friend, which might have caused her indigestion. She woke up the next day with a bloated stomach and a slight headache. A week later, she went to a friend's birthday party and had diarrhea after drinking wine and beer. Two weeks later, she traveled to Busan and went to a place called "Cheongsapo," which had the best grilled seafood.

I feel terrible for the patient, but I do not have the time to listen to these words. There are many respiratory patients in the waiting room, and what makes me even more anxious is that a patient is waiting for a bronchoscopy procedure. I have no choice but to interrupt the patient.

"What symptom is bothering you the most right now?"

The expression on the patient's face changes dramatically. The sparrow near a school sings the primer. This means that, regardless of how little knowledge or experience you have, if you stay in a field long enough, you will gain some knowledge and experience. I am naturally quite observant. I have been seeing patients for 30 years. If you could count the number of times I have met with patients, it would likely be well over two million. I cannot help but notice when patients feel upset.

After seeing the patient, I thought, since she was angry, she might speak unfavorably about my clinic to her friends and acquaintances, and if that did not make her feel better, she would leave "bad reviews" on the Internet.

Consequently, I become nervous and worried when I see a young female patient in her 20s. The first thing that comes to mind when someone is diagnosed with a cold is that I feel sorry for them because I know the visit will end soon. This patient appeared very young, but she was in her 30s. What a relief! Female patients in their 30s are technically considered millennials or Generation Zs, but they tend to be less intense than those in their 20s. I hope readers do not get the wrong impression of me. I am not trying to start a debate on sexism or generational conflict. I am speaking from my own experience, not from any scientific or objective data or evidence, and talking about my personal impressions.

I am sharing this story because this patient's question brought back many memories for me, giving me an opportunity to reflect on myself. After a diagnosis following a brief questioning, I gave her a prescription for medication and told her to come back if she was uncomfortable. This was when she asked me a question out of nowhere.

"By the way, doctor, why Anam-dong?"

I was momentarily stumped. What did she say? What does it mean? That night, I thought about Anam-dong.

Anam-dong.
The meaning of the Chinese characters is "an" for comfort, "am" for rock, and "dong" for neighborhood. Together, this means a comfortable neighborhood with rocks.
Anam-dong has been an area of great interest for feng shui since the fourth year of King Taejo of the Joseon Dynasty in 1395 because of its beautiful and outstanding scenery. Originally, the name "anam" is said to have originated from a large rock in the Daegwang Apartment Complex in Anam-dong 3-ga, where approximately 20 people could sit and rest comfortably. The rock was called the "comfortable sitting rock," which was written using the Chinese character "anam."

Anam-dong is home to "Korea University," one of the oldest and top-ranked universities in South Korea, as well as to "Sungshin Women's University," "Yongmun Middle and High Schools," and "Anam Elementary School."

I have strong ties to Seongbuk-gu, where Anam-dong is located. Dongseon-dong, which is close to Anam-dong, is my home base. I was born in the neighborhood. I was born in Dongseon-dong, Seongbuk-gu. It was fate that I opened my clinic at 98-1 anam-dong 2-ga, or 8 Goryeo-daero 13-gil, under the current address system.

I have changed jobs only once in my life. My first job was at the now-closed Seoul Baek Hospital, the parent organization of Inje University College of Medicine, located at Euljiro 3-ga, Jung-gu, Seoul. The Beautiful Breath Clinic in Anam-dong is my second job. I worked at my first job from 1994 to early February 2001 and at my second job from February 26, 2001, to 2024, for a total of 23 years in one place.

They say that the rivers and mountains change in 10 years, and over the past 23 years the clinic has expanded four times in one location in Anam-dong to become the Beautiful Breath Clinic today. From a small internal medicine clinic that opened on February 26, 2001, in a 27-square-foot space with only two employees, a nurse and a clinical pathologist, the clinic has grown into a medical center with 20 employees in a 200-square-foot space.

Anam-dong is my home, where I have devoted all my time, from my 30s to my 50s, to work. It is a melting pot of my life's challenges and failures, accomplishments and joys, hurts and wounds.

Just as the ancestors of the Joseon Dynasty considered Anam-dong to be a place of beautiful feng shui and comfortable rocks, it has been the most comfortable and sturdy rock of my life, even after more than 600 years. People from all over South Korea and overseas visit our clinic in Anam-dong. On the corner of a two-lane road, the building is old but built on a comfortable rock.

When this building was first built, there was a large boulder in the basement, making it a true treasure built on a rock.

A boulder is a broad, flat rock.

The word "rock" is popular in Christianity, symbolically referring to "God" as a protector and refuge and "Jesus Christ" as the firm foundation of salvation.

During my 23 years of treating critically ill and emergency patients, I felt an invisible "care" or "blessing." My life is not that of an ordinary physician. As a doctor, I have come to where I am today by struggling and giving everything I have, with the "belief" that saving people's lives is what makes a doctor a true doctor.

Even with the blessing of oblivion from God, more than 30 scenes of struggling with a dying patient alone survive in my memory and unfold like a panorama. Some of them were almost brought back to life from death.

There were patients whose hearts stopped, their oxygen saturation was zero, and their skin color turned grayish, resembling a corpse. I have also stopped while performing CPR, covered in cold sweat and thinking the patient was dead.

I have had many "moments of awe" as I watched their hearts miraculously start beating again, their oxygen levels rise from zero to 30%, 50%, 90%, and their gray skin turn pink.

I am a physician who specializes in medicine, among other natural sciences. Medicine trusts cause and effect and does not accept beliefs without supporting evidence.

It rejects superstition and despises witchcraft. However, I believe that the Beautiful Breath Clinic, which has been built on the old rock of Anam-dong, has been blessed by the heavens. Medicine is all about statistics. Whatever happens in the realm of medicine is purely based on statistics, rather than a coincidence.

What are statistics?

Statistics are numbers that reflect specific quantitative descriptions of collective phenomena. It is the science of numerical representation of the situation of social or natural populations. The "cost of living for the population of Seoul," the "production of semiconductors in South

Korea," and the number of defective products in the "sample" are some examples.

Statistics are about populations. Therefore, a numerical description such as a person's wealth or the height of a mountain is not a statistic, no matter how specific. Modern social life and science would not exist without statistics.

A medical procedure is considered invasive if any part of the test equipment enters the tissues of the body. Examples of invasive tests include blood tests using "needles," biopsies, gastroscopy, colonoscopy, and bronchoscopy.

All endoscopic procedures have potential adverse events. There are medical statistics on the adverse events of an "endoscopy," the types of side effects that can occur when undergoing gastroscopy, and the frequency (%) at which they occur. I often use statistics on the type and frequency of adverse events associated with bronchoscopy.

Statistics are frequencies over a population, so naturally, the larger the population, the larger the count. The number of adverse events seen in ten bronchoscopies is not the same as the frequency seen in 100 bronchoscopies.

I have performed the most "bronchoscopies" in South Korea. Once one has successfully performed 200 bronchoscopies on 200 patients, they are certified as a bronchoscopy specialist. I have met this requirement hundreds of times.

The frequency of complications is inevitably high, including some very serious ones. This may not necessarily be related to the skill of the doctor performing the procedure. Unforeseen complications can also arise. One cannot predict an unknown drug allergy in a patient. It is not the fault of the doctor or the patient, but an incident that can arise suddenly, like a natural disaster.

As a young, energetic man, when I saw critically ill patients, I took great pride in being able to keep them safe with emergency care.

The boughs that bear the most fruit hang the lowest. Now, I know quite well that I have not saved dying patients because I am good.

Of the critically ill and emergency patients I see and treat every day, thankfully, not a single one has died at our hospital.
This is a miracle that is solely due to God's blessings upon Anam-dong, which is built on a rock. I made it through another day of emergency and critical care without any casualties. I will do it again tomorrow.

To me, Anam-dong is the promised land of blessings.

God bless Abam-dong!
Forever!

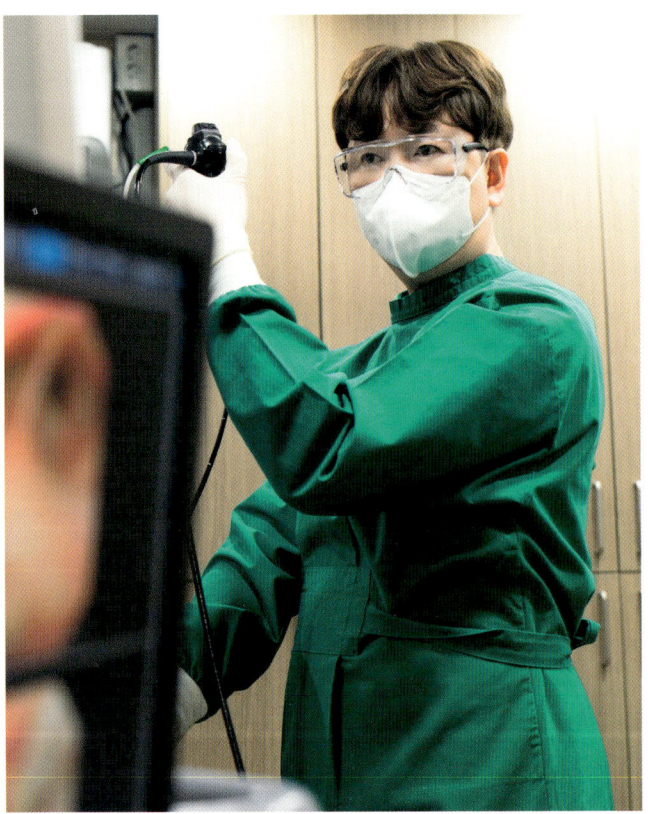

Dr. SEONGLIM JIN, Director of the Beautiful Breath Clinic, performing a bronchoscopy.

04
Can you enjoy your life?

I have been a cheerful, bubbly goofball since I was a child. Even before I started elementary school, I was notorious in my neighborhood for being a troublemaker, making noise, and getting into trouble. Each day, when the morning dawned, my mother would say, "Please behave yourself today."

However, don't you know that people do not change easily? Do you believe an eight-year-old child is truly capable of reflecting on his innate tendencies and independently resolving his issues?

My extremely outgoing, mischievous, and playful demeanor continued through sixth grade.

Looking back, I realize how enjoyable it was to be a goofball and have a good time at school.

I was happy. I spent my days playing soccer, baseball, hopscotch, squid, tag, red light-green light, stick tossing, slap match, and marbles; running away after ringing the doorbell at other people's houses; picking dates at other people's houses; playing with fire in the backyard; catching sparrows with a slingshot; cutting elastic bands when the girls were playing with them; and doing countless other fun things.

Fifty years later, I still have vivid memories of those days. The skies were blue, with cotton candy clouds. There was no such thing as a personal computer, and the concept of a mobile phone had not even been conceived.

I ran around all day, hunted for arrowroot in the mountains, and stirred up the entire neighborhood. I grew up in a place called Galhyeondong, Eunpyeong-gu, Gangbuk. It was not until I entered high school that I gradually became more introverted. After puberty, my ability to think and empathize began to blossom.

I opened my eyes to the hardships of life earlier than the pleasures of life, trying to find answers to religious and philosophical questions such as "Why are humans born, live for a while, and then leave, and where do they go after they die?," while listening to pop songs played on MBC radio every night.

During medical school, I buried myself in a vast collection of medical books. I was the first student to arrive at the library at around 5 a.m. and the last to leave in the evening.

I studied alone in the library, even on Chuseok Eve, Chuseok Day, Christmas Eve, and Christmas Day. I found learning about the mysterious human body very interesting. In short, the rigors of medical school were not an obligation for me but a pleasure.

Throughout my six years of medical school, I maintained top grades. My nickname at the time was "a walking Harrison."

Harrison was like the Bible of internal medicine textbooks, a very large textbook of internal medicine knowledge, about 10,000 pages in the original English with volumes 1 and 2 combined.

After completing my internship and four years of residency, I chose pulmonology as my full-time specialty. When I began practicing pulmonology, I forgot my basic inclination to enjoy life.

I could not enjoy my life. My heart was filled with sadness and compassion as I saw the plight of critically ill respiratory patients and the tears of their families as they struggled with the daily battle between life and death.

Even then, I did not even remotely consider the idea that my life would be consumed by "obligations and responsibilities." After completing my residency, I began my life in pulmonology as a full-time lecturer and assistant professor.

In 2000, an unprecedented collective action by doctors as a part of the dispensing separation led to financial difficulties for the hospital.

The board of directors cut the salaries of professors by 50% without prior consultation or consent. I was shocked. I wanted to practice, research, and teach in pulmonology until I retired from the hospital at my alma mater.

I was never hungry for money. Turning a blind eye to my sincerity, the board unilaterally cut the salaries of faculty members who were not unionized at the time. I was angry. I felt betrayed. The money-grubbing behavior of the hospital was appalling. I made up my mind. I decided that I needed to open my own practice to legitimately make my own and not other people's money. After that decision, I began searching around Seoul for a good place to open my practice. Even 23 years ago, there was no place to open a clinic in Seoul because the best spots were already occupied.

After seeing an advertisement for a clinic for lease in the classified section of the Doctors News, a newspaper for doctors, in the new city of Buksuwon, I visited the site. I liked the building as it was in a clean neighborhood in the center of a new city. I signed the contract right away and moved my house to Bundang, preparing to open a clinic in the new city of Buksuwon.

It was the Lunar New Year 2001. At a gathering of relatives, my aunt, who was a professor at Sungkyunkwan University at the time, shared the news that a branch of Samsung Medical Center would be opening in Buksuwon. Samsung Medical Center was the first hospital affiliated with a major conglomerate to integrate a corporate service ethos into a university hospital. I was stuck. I did not feel comfortable competing directly with Samsung Medical Center.

Returning home at 8 p.m. after the gathering ended, I browsed through the classified ads in Doctors News for a clinic for lease again and found a listing for a small building in Anam-dong.

When I arrived, I saw that a Korea University Hospital was nearby, but no apartment complexes around, just old hanoks and row houses. I looked around, saw the current occupancy of the small building, met with the owner, and called it a day.

I decided to give up the location in Buksuwon. I also gave up my KRW 40 million down payment. The building in Buksuwon was scheduled for completion in September 2001, with plans to open a clinic there in October. Meanwhile, the Anam-dong building was set to be ready for a clinic opening by late February 2001.

I decided it was okay to forgo the KRW 40 million down payment if I could open my clinic seven months earlier. Anam-dong is a neighborhood with a rural feel and kind-hearted residents in the surrounding area. I thought it would be a great place to spread a good reputation through word of mouth. It is a central neighborhood in Seoul with a rural spirit.

I researched which physicians Anam-dong residents usually saw. In their words, I sensed their desire to have an internal medicine clinic in the Anam-dong area.

As I met with residents like a congressman campaigning for an election, I was convinced that I could start a successful practice in Anam-dong. That was how I opened SEONGLIM JIN Clinic on February 26, 2001.

Five years later, on September 1, 2006, the clinic was renamed the Beautiful Breath Clinic, specializing in pulmonology. Equipped with CT equipment, white light bronchoscopy equipment, and fluorescence bronchoscopy equipment, it became the first primary care clinic for pulmonologists to perform
bronchoscopy in South Korea.

The clinic received many awards, including the first "title" of a private practice as a primary care facility, and a citation from the "Minister of Health and Welfare" for its dedication to the treatment of pulmonary tuberculosis patients. It has been a long 18 years since I started performing bronchoscopy in a primary care setting.

In my private practice, which is classified as a primary care clinic in the healthcare delivery system, I treated patients with respiratory diseases that were overwhelming for a clinic, through biopsy of lung cancer, removal of foreign bodies in the bronchi, removal and treatment of purulent sputum stuck like a foreign body in bronchiectasis, diagnosis and treatment of bronchial tuberculosis, diagnosis of lung cancer, evaluation of asthma assessment level 1, COPD assessment level 1, and designation as a healthcare institution for the treatment of latent tuberculosis. As the years passed, I became completely drained from treating critically ill respiratory patients.

As I walked the path of a pioneer in private practice, I was faced with various regulations and interference, such as the scrutiny of reviewers and audits by Health Insurance Review and Assessment (HIRA) and Service and Ministry of Health and Welfare, which made my first attempt at diagnosis and treatment difficult and unenjoyable.

I wondered whether I could quit the clinic and take a break, but something would not let me go: my sense of duty and responsibility. There was no escape from the wave of patients with unresolved respiratory diseases coming from all over the country and the world, including Haenam, Jejudo, Ulleungdo, Mokpo, Busan, Daegu, Daejeon, Cheongju, Cheongju, Gangneung, Gyeongju, Mungyeong, Wando, Yeosu, Gunsan, Jeonju, Jinju, Geoje, all areas of Gyeonggido and Seoul, the United States, Canada, China, Japan, Thailand, Malaysia, Singapore, Germany, and Italy.

My body began to ache.

> "For those who enjoy their work, the world is heaven;
> for those who regard work as a duty, the world is hell."
>
> - Leonardo da Vinci

This quote by Leonardo da Vinci emphasizes the importance of having fun while working. Leonardo da Vinci must have been a genius to realize this truth so long ago.

Then I realized, a quote from an ancient genius is only as good as the words of his time. As a pulmonologist running a legendary private practice in South Korea, I have to bear that weight even if the place I consider my duty and work is hell on earth.

I believe that my sense of duty to my patients and responsibility to the people in our clinic is the fundamental reason I was put on this earth, even if I do not always enjoy what I do. I do not know how much longer I can carry this weight, obligation, and responsibility. However, I will not stop here. I am a pulmonologist who is desperately needed by patients with respiratory diseases.

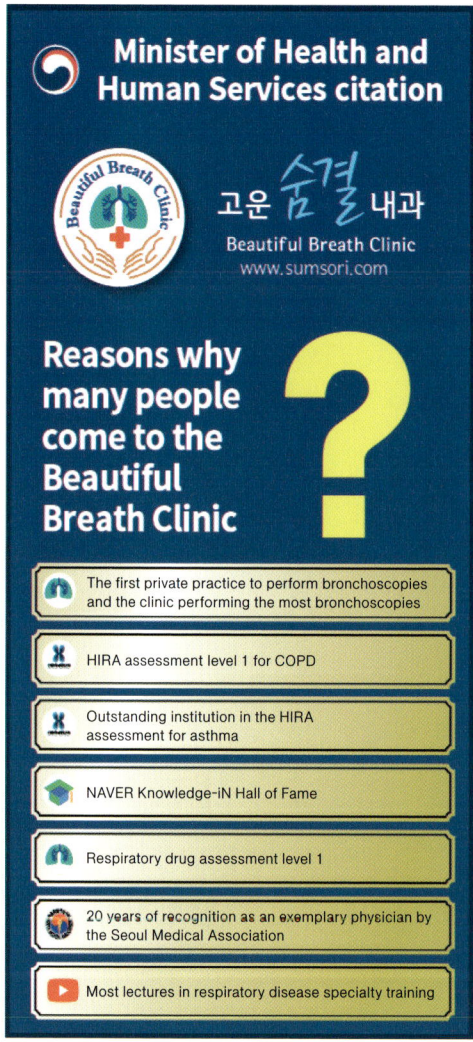

Minister of Health and Human Services citation and other awards for the Beautiful Breath Clinic.

05
Fate determined in a "split second"

I am a pulmonologist. As a specialist in an essential healthcare discipline, I diagnose and treat various diseases of the human respiratory system.
Consider a patient with pain due to stomach inflammation or a stomach ulcer. This pain can range from mild to unbearable, depending on the severity of the disease.
Now consider an acute exacerbation of asthma causing shortness of breath. Stomach ulcers and gastritis do not pose an immediate threat to life. It is usually treated with stomach ulcer medications, injections, or gastritis medications. However, an acute exacerbation of asthma is a very serious and life-threatening condition. Without prompt diagnosis and quick treatment by a specialist, the patient could die. Pulmonologists often see such emergencies and know how critical every second is.

The Korean word chalna, which originated from the Sanskrit word kṣaṇa, means a split second when an event or phenomenon occurs and is a Buddhist-derived term for the smallest unit of time. I would like to begin this story by recalling the memories of that day when my life and destiny were decided in such a split second.
August 2021 was the height of the COVID-19 pandemic.
I was doing my customary work at the hospital. Around 11:00 a.m., I felt uncomfortable, like I was having indigestion. I skipped lunch. By 3 p.m., I was feeling nauseous and had pain in the area around my belly button.

Upon returning home from the clinic, the pain in my stomach moved to my right lower abdomen and was very severe. I was experiencing excruciating abdominal pain that prevented me from extending my back, and the pain increased when I released my hand compared to when I pressed on my right lower abdominal area. A finding that pain increases when releasing the hand compared to pressing on the area of pain is medically known as rebound tenderness and is often associated with a serious condition that requires emergency medical attention and surgery.

"Oops!" A diagnosis ran through my head. It was "acute appendicitis." Acute appendicitis is an acute inflammation of the appendix, an anatomical area on the large intestine called the appendix protuberance, and is most often treated surgically.

I went to the emergency room at the hospital. The emergency physician's first diagnosis was "acute appendicitis," as expected. I was immediately sent for an abdominal CT scan. Emergency surgery was withheld based on the finding that the appendix was very distended and on the verge of rupture, but it did not appear to have ruptured. I was scheduled for surgery the next morning and spent the evening and that night on antibiotics and pain medication injections while awaiting surgery the next day.

At 11 p.m., my temperature spiked to 40°C degrees. My entire body was shaking like a leaf, and the pain in my abdomen was unbearable. I have never experienced such intense pain in my life. My intestines felt like they were going to be ripped out, and my entire abdomen felt like it was being cooked in a pot of boiling water. I received several fever reducer injections and nonsteroidal anti-inflammatory drug (NSAID) injections.

My fever was persistent, and by 2 a.m., my blood pressure had dropped. As a physician, I knew instinctively that my condition was deteriorating.

However, I could not get emergency surgery at 2 a.m. We were in the midst of the COVID-19 pandemic, which did not allow for emergency surgery for patients like me. My surgery was scheduled for 9 a.m.

There were still seven hours left, after spending the previous seven hours in constant stomach pain,

I entered the operation room. I have never had general anesthesia before. As I lay on the operating table, waiting for general anesthesia, I was reminded of my days as an intern 30 years ago, when I moved more than 10 patients a day onto the operating table.

Without giving it much thought, I had placed patients on the operating table. Without thinking, I helped with the pre-anesthesia preparation. As a patient, I could finally put myself in their shoes and understand their anxiety and fear. "Walk in other people's shoes" means that you can understand someone only if you put yourself in their place. It was not until I experienced general anesthesia myself that I understood the fears of patients undergoing surgery under general anesthesia.

After 30 years of being in the dark, I finally understood the patient's anxiety in a whirlwind of emotions. I did not remember how the surgery ended. The faint voices in my hazy consciousness disturbed me even more.

The conversation between the anesthesiologist and the nurse was full of medical terms and jargon, but as a doctor, I knew exactly what they meant.

"Why is his blood pressure so low?"

"His oxygen levels aren't rising either."

"The arterial blood gas analysis (ABGA) shows an oxygen tension of 70 mmHg.

Uh! What?

As a pulmonologist, I was shocked to hear that my arterial blood oxygen partial pressure was 70 mmHg. The normal value of arterial oxygen tension is 90 mmHg to 99 mmHg. To make matters worse, I knew that my body's arterial blood oxygen partial pressure of 70 mmHg while on oxygen after surgery indicated a very serious condition.

Simply put, for the sake of readers, it means that I was supplied with oxygen, but the supplied oxygen was not reaching my lungs properly.

If your lungs do not get enough oxygen, you die. If you are not dead, you are braindead.

Surgery for common appendicitis has few complications. Modern appendicitis surgery is no longer done through an open abdominal incision as in the past, but through a small hole in the abdomen for the entry of a laparoscope.

There are many advantages to non-open surgery, but the most important is that there are fewer adverse events in the respiratory system. However, the readings on my tests were indicating something was wrong with my lungs.

This jolted me as a physician who had spent 23 years as a pulmonologist. It did not take me long to realize that it was not just a problem with my lungs. Back in the ward, my blood pressure was 70 mm Hg systolic and only 40 mm Hg diastolic. This indicated very severe hypotension. My heart rate was over 140 beats per minute.

I could have a heart attack any minute. After surgery for appendicitis, the body temperature should return to normal. It would make sense that, since the source of the inflammation, appendicitis, has been surgically removed, my temperature would return to normal.

However, my body temperature fluctuated between 39 and 40°C. My body temperature increased, my blood pressure decreased, my heart rate increased, and my oxygen tension reduced. The results of my post-operative blood tests shocked me even more.

My white blood cell count was 29,000 (17,000-18,000 for severe inflammation or pneumonia; 4,000-8,000 for normal) and 92% of my white blood cells were "neutrophils."

In short, my body was much more inflamed than in the pre-operative state of my appendicitis, which meant that the inflammation was spreading throughout my body. The surgeon who led the operation came. I asked him to increase the dose of the antibiotic I was currently on to the maximum dose.

I told him that, based on my condition after the surgery, it could be sepsis. However, the surgeon did not agree with me and explained that the surgery went very well. He said this can happen temporarily and that blood tests sometimes show such results after surgery.

The surgeon took my hand and said, "Dear patient, do not believe the test results; trust me, the surgery went well."
These words still give me goosebumps when I think about them.
Those words will stay with me for the rest of my life as a doctor. I never said the surgery had gone wrong. The surgeon must have said that the surgery went well from the perspective of a surgeon. However, he said so on the basis of his own visual observations. Various signs and test findings after surgery indicated that I, the patient, was dying.
I do not intend to badmouth or criticize the surgeon who operated on me. I was not an ordinary patient but a pulmonologist who had seen, diagnosed, and treated countless patients in dangerous situations with severe illnesses, all the while managing their lives.
It would have been safe and reasonable for the surgeon to give it a second thought if the patient, who happened to be a physician and a key player in essential healthcare, had raised a question.

Now, there was only one way for me to survive. I knew that if I did not try here, I would not last a day. I made a scene in the ward. I screamed like a madman. I frantically yelled at the nurse to increase the antibiotics to the maximum dose immediately. Out of hope that if I did this, the surgeon would come back and treat me properly, I raved like a lunatic.
However, the surgeon never came back. Instead of the surgeon who performed the operation, a psychiatrist came. The nurses stood by my side with sedatives and sleeping pills ready to put me to sleep. The nurses looked like the Grim Reaper.
Sepsis is a very scary disease with a 40% fatality rate. Bacteria swirl around in the blood and destroy various organs, eventually leading to death. The only way to treat sepsis is to administer the maximum dose of antibiotics quickly and without delay. However, if patients with sepsis are given sedatives to put them to sleep, rather than the full dose of antibiotics they need, they will die.

By the time the psychiatrist arrived, I was already in a near-death state, unconscious, short of breath, and unable to move my head. I knew that if I failed to convince the psychiatrist, I would die. I was in that split second between life and death.

I did everything in my power to convince the psychiatrist with medical logic. I convinced the psychiatrist that I was indeed septic and not suffering from delirium, which could occur after surgery, and it was no post-operative anxiety or panic disorder either.

Now, my life was no longer in the hands of the surgeon who operated on me but in those of the psychiatrist.
Thankfully, this was not how my life ended. The psychiatrist listened to me and told the surgeon that I was not delirious, and I was finally given the maximum dose of antibiotics. Six hours passed after administering the maximum dose of antibiotics. My blood pressure, temperature, arterial blood oxygen partial pressure, and heart rate returned to normal.

I was brought back from the very brink of death.
Doctors diagnose and treat patients. A wrong diagnosis leads to the wrong treatment. Even with proper diagnosis and treatment, a patient's condition can worsen. In many cases, it is beyond our control.
However, this experience makes all doctors, including myself, take a moment to reflect. If I had not been a pulmonologist, an essential healthcare specialist treating critically ill patients, I would have died.
Two days later, the surgical biopsy report said "acute," meaning that it progresses quickly, and "suppurative," meaning that it had become pus-like. The word "appendicitis" means inflammation of the appendix (the tip of the cecum).
"Microperforation" refers to a hole that cannot be seen by the human eye. The bacteria had already spread into the blood through the hole. The cause of sepsis was medically identified.
August 15, 2021. I'll never forget those glorious clear skies and clouds. After enduring and surviving the struggle for two days, I went back to

the Beautiful Breath Clinic. I could not just take a leisurely break with so many patients waiting for me. I started seeing patients at the clinic while receiving antibiotic injections.

As of March 2024, we are reliving the pain of the healthcare crisis. The situation was sparked by the government's announcement to increase medical school enrollment by 2,000 students at once to revitalize essential healthcare.

Essential healthcare is a very serious matter, with the lives of people and the security of nations at stake. It is imperative to understand why top healthcare talent is avoiding essential healthcare. People know it.

The work is hard with little reward. Such rewards are not about healthcare alone. The only thing left for doctors specializing in essential healthcare in this era is a sense of mission. It is the last bastion of pride.

It begs the question: who is taking down the last bastion of doctors dedicated to essential healthcare?

06
One word to live by

Through the years as a pulmonologist, I have seen more than 110,000 first-time patients (those who come to the hospital for the first time). The number of 110,000 first-time patients and more than 2 million revisits is phenomenal. No single physician in private practice has seen more respiratory disease than I have.

The laws of statistics apply to diseases. Seeing more respiratory patients means seeing more patients with very severe cases of any respiratory disease. I do not have a detailed memory of patients with mild colds or well-controlled asthma.

However, I remember the patients who were suffering from very severe illnesses, or those that took a significant time and effort to be treated, from the first time I met them to when they were well treated and their condition was under control.

This is similar to the course of a romantic relationship. When two people meet each other, develop good feelings, and start dating, they remember the day they first met and celebrate their one-year anniversary together, right? They celebrate and remember each other's birthdays, and Christmas. For Valentine's Day on February 14, women give chocolates or gifts to men they like, and for White Day on March 14, men give candy or gifts to women they like.

In the doctor-patient relationship, meeting a patient and building trust and working together to heal them is like meeting a life partner or a lover.

Similar to friendships and romantic relationships, the doctor-patient relationship can be joyful, rewarding, and full of gratitude. Sometimes there are conflicting emotions and breakups. Some patients may return over a hundred times, while others may visit only once. Other patients you see once and never forget.

The first appearance of a patient when he walked into my office in March 2024 has been imprinted on my brain. A male patient in his 70s was holding a portable oxygen concentrator in one hand and a chest tube drainage in the other. Just by looking at him, I could tell that he was suffering from very severe respiratory distress. His face was pale, he was gasping for air, and I could hear crackles (indicating sputum in the alveoli) and wheezes (indicating bronchial narrowing) even without a stethoscope.

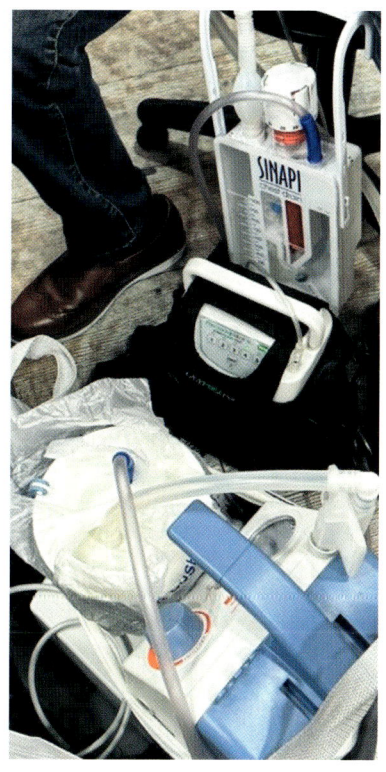

Photograph of a patient with a chest tube drainage and a portable oxygen concentrator.

Even more surprising was the fact that the chest tube drainage weighed more than 20 kg and the portable oxygen tanks more than 10 kg. He would have been out of breath from walking even without the two barrels, but he was carrying the two devices himself.

He came in unaccompanied. How hard would that be? How much trouble did he go through? My heart was filled with sadness and compassion. I did a simple chest x-ray, basic blood work, and oximetry.

A simple chest radiograph showed a pneumothorax (a tear in the pleura with air compressing the lung) and empyema (pus in the pleura enclosing the lung) in the left lung. The left lung was almost non-functional, and the right lung was in a state of compensatory hyperinflation (human breathing requires the right and left lungs to work equally.

Compensatory hyperinflation means that when one lung loses function, the other lung has to work harder, causing it to enlarge with stretched alveoli.
Even with a pneumothorax, breathing is difficult. Empyema causes shortness of breath, constant sputum production, and infection. When both are present in the same lung at the same time, it is hard to imagine the difficulty in breathing, chest pain, and pain from the pus-like sputum.
Even after being treated with antibiotics at a university hospital, the pus-like sputum continued to bother the patient. He was clutching at straws when he came to the Beautiful Breath Clinic after being treated at a university hospital.
However, his critical condition did not allow me to perform a bronchoscopy to remove the very heavy sputum in his bronchi. With a pneumothorax and empyema and a chest tube intubation, bronchoscopy to clear the sputum was not only risky but also futile as the symptoms would continue without resolving the pre-existing pneumothorax and empyema.
I explained this to the patient, who looked disappointed and disheartened. He realized that his attempt at clutching the last straw had been pointless.

"I have been wanting to meet with you, doctor, since a year ago, and today, after seeing you, I have no regrets. My wish has been granted."

My heart sank and tears welled up in my eyes.
How much pain and suffering had he endured? With his condition

persisting despite repeated procedures and antibiotics, he said he had been wanting to come to the Beautiful Breath Clinic since a year ago. He finally made it after circumstances prevented him from doing so before. He came to the clinic as his last resort, where his hopes were shattered.

This was the most heartbreaking moment as a doctor.

I felt helpless and extremely sorry for the patient. It would have been a much more normal reaction to complain or get angry about why I could not cure his disease. Instead, the patient said he had no regrets and that his wishes had been granted. The patient's words will remain unforgettable and touch my heart for the rest of my life. It will constantly question me and remind me of the mindset

I need to maintain for my patients. The day-to-day practice of a pulmonologist can be very demanding, lonely, and exhausting.

Late at night, I often lie awake imagining the bronchoscopies that I will be performing on critically ill patients the next day. I have spent not just 1 but 23 years of my life like this.

I was tired of the struggle, depression, and fatigue that I had not felt in my 30s. The fact that I will soon be in my 60s reminds me not only of the impermanence of time but also that I am becoming physically exhausted through my aches and pains.

There are many times when I want to quit, take a break, and let it all go. However, I know my patients expect me to continue to fulfill my professional role with all my heart and strength.

Although I cannot address many serious conditions, I can address many others. The sense of reward and mission I feel when I resolve a problem is what keeps me going. It is hard to let go of the heavy burden of essential care that I carry when I learn how my patients feel, even in those moments when I have not been able to treat a serious illness.

Every day is difficult and every moment is tense and stressful, but I know that my life as a pulmonologist who has chosen "essential healthcare" can be sustained by the comfort from the simple words "It's okay, good job!"

For 23 years, I have lived a life of hard work, passion, and integrity. I probably have about 10 years of work ahead of me. No. The idea that I have a decade or so ahead of me may also be wrong.

We never know when our lives will end. However, I cannot rest because the moment I meet a patient with a respiratory disease, the notion that I have lived my life with such intensity and challenges that I have earned the right to rest disappears in an instant.

As long patients are struggling, sick, and out of breath, I will continue to do what I can. That is the foundation that enables me to say, "I'm Dr. SEONGLIM JIN, a pulmonologist."

Chapter 2

Unimaginable pain of shortness of breath

Characteristics of fatal pneumonia and pneumonia in older adults

Is Seoul National University Hospital the best option?

Sincerity is the way of Heaven

Diagnoses lie in the words of patients

01
Unimaginable pain of shortness of breath

To borrow a Buddhist concept, life is an ocean full of conflict and pain. This means that human life is marked by suffering from birth. Even in the Bible, human life is a process of suffering, as Adam and Eve ate the fruit from the tree of the knowledge of good and evil. There is also a phrase describing life as "joy, anger, sorrow, and happiness." This means that life is a process of experiencing various emotions. "What professionals most commonly encounter human suffering?" Doctors.
Among doctors, pulmonologists, who diagnose and treat respiratory diseases, see a great deal of human suffering. There are many different respiratory diseases, and patients will experience different symptoms such as cough, sputum, chest pain, and shortness of breath. Among these symptoms lies suffering that readers cannot imagine.

Even as a respiratory physician, I cannot imagine the difficulty of breathing with one of these conditions. I just try to understand the pain through the words of the patient. How can I explain it in writing if I have never experienced it firsthand?
Could it be like the shortness of breath after sprinting a hundred meters? Could it be like the shortness of breath after running a marathon? Could it be like the shortness of breath when drowning? I cannot express it sufficiently well.
I wish I could be a linguistic genius and communicate the nature of such shortness of breath. What kind of respiratory disease could cause this terrifying shortness of breath?
Pulmonary fibrosis. Although an unfamiliar diagnosis, pulmonary

fibrosis has been rapidly increasing in recent years. For an accurate understanding of pulmonary fibrosis, the anatomical location of the respiratory tract must be understood. The clinical classification of respiratory diseases based on anatomical location is as follows.

1) Airway and bronchial diseases: Bronchial asthma, bronchiectasis.
2) Diseases of the alveoli: Pneumonia, lung cancer
3) Interstitial lung disease: Pulmonary fibrosis

Interstitial compartment means the space in between. A disease that occurs in the anatomical location between the bronchi and alveoli is called interstitial lung disease.

Pulmonary fibrosis is the most common and important respiratory disease in the interstitial compartment. A common symptom of pulmonary fibrosis is shortness of breath; however, many respiratory conditions that can cause this. Bronchial asthma, a well-known respiratory disease, also causes shortness of breath.
However, shortness of breath in bronchial asthma is different from that in pulmonary fibrosis. The shortness of breath in asthma is characterized by diurnal fluctuations, meaning that the symptoms come and go over the course of a 24-hour day. Shortness of breath may appear in the morning and at night but disappear during the day. The shortness of breath in pulmonary fibrosis does not fluctuate; patients are out of breath all day. This shortness of breath becomes more severe when walking and worsens when climbing stairs or hills.
In the early stages, pulmonary fibrosis has no symptoms, making early detection difficult. Even when symptoms are present, they are often mistaken for asthma or bronchitis. If one goes to the doctor with symptoms, the doctor must suspect pulmonary fibrosis and run various tests to make an accurate diagnosis.
By the time it is detected on a simple chest radiograph, pulmonary fibrosis has often progressed quite a bit. If pulmonary fibrosis is delayed in diagnosis or left untreated, complications can arise. Common complications of pulmonary fibrosis include the following:

1) Respiratory failure
2) Lung Cancer
3) Pulmonary arterial hypertension
4) Pneumonia
5) Multiple organ failure

Respiratory failure causes death as the lungs are unable to perform their normal function of taking in oxygen and exchanging it with carbon dioxide. Patients can develop lung cancer or even go into multiple organ failure, in which their liver or kidneys fail.
What causes dreaded pulmonary fibrosis? The most common causes still remain unknown.

Unknown cause?

Yes, the cause is most often unknown. If no cause can be identified, the disease is called idiopathic pulmonary fibrosis. This is important among the types of interstitial lung disease owing to its poor prognosis and commonness. The diagnosis of this disease can be made as follows:
1) Simple chest radiograph
2) High-resolution chest CT or low-dose chest CT
3) Pulmonary function tests (PFTs): Restrictive ventilatory defect, decreased DLco (decreased lung diffusing capacity
4) Bronchoscopy: Bronchoalveolar lavage (BAL)
5) Blood tests: KL6 test (new medical technology)
6) Lung biopsy

Two medications are available to treat idiopathic pulmonary fibrosis. Since the cause is fibrosis of the lungs, antifibrotic drugs that slow down the rate at which fibrosis progresses are the most important treatment. No antifibrotic drugs existed 20 years ago, as the world's first was developed 10 years ago.

Pirfenidone (trade name: Pirespa®) and nintedanib (trade name:

OFEV®) are the currently available drugs. Pirfenidone is covered by insurance, but nintedanib is not as of April 2024. Pirfenidone is associated with many adverse events, the most common of which are as follows:
1) Digestive disorders
2) Liver dysfunction
3) Photosensitized skin inflammation
4) 50% reduced drug blood levels from smoking
5) Increased drug concentration when taken with grapefruit juice

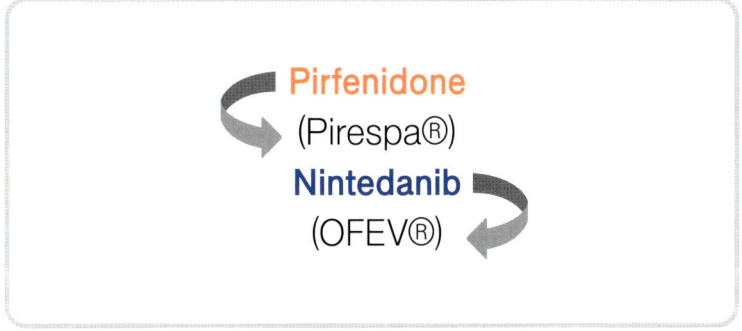

Medications for pulmonary fibrosis.

A 75-year-old man presented with shortness of breath and a cough. He started having symptoms three years ago and was diagnosed with bronchial asthma and COPD at another hospital, where he was treated with steroid inhalers and inhaled bronchodilators. However, his symptoms did not improve, and two weeks ago his shortness of breath became very severe.

His symptoms should have improved if the diagnosis of bronchial asthma and COPD had been correct. Except in special cases, the combination of proper diagnosis and treatment improves the patient's condition.
In this patient's case, many factors could have led to a misdiagnosis.

Unfortunately, when a certain combination of diagnosis and treatment fails, it is necessary to revisit the cause to determine the validity of the initial diagnosis and other factors that could be causing the patient's symptoms. This patient did not, in fact, have bronchial asthma but had idiopathic pulmonary fibrosis.

The danger of a misdiagnosis is that the actual disease may progress and the time for treatment may be missed.

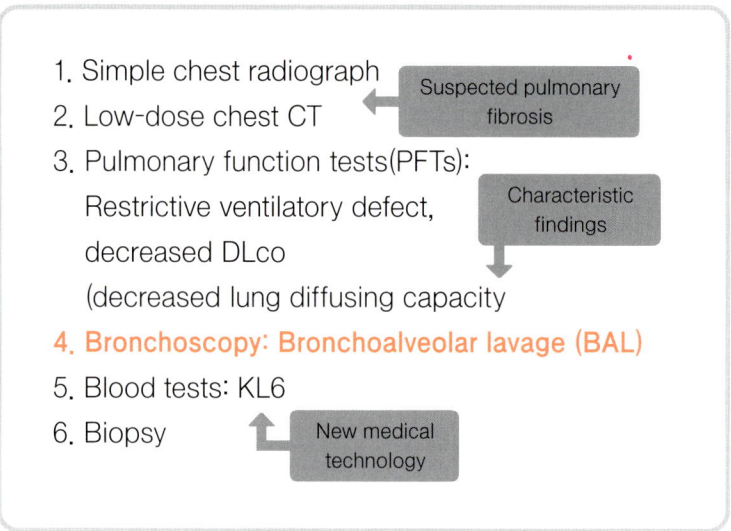

Medications for pulmonary fibrosis.

The initial diagnosis by a doctor is very important. Doctors refer to the perception they have before that first diagnosis as an impression. An impression is a physiological change that an external stimulus imprints on the body. When diagnosing a condition in which the body is pathologically altered by a cause, the condition before providing the final diagnosis is called an impression.

Physicians need to make these impressions well. This is why internal medicine is often referred to as the "flower of medicine."

The final diagnosis must be made by a physician using impressions to determine the course of treatment: whether to treat it with medication or surgery, or what medication, at what dose, and for how many days. If surgery is needed, the surgery needs to be determined and a referral to the appropriate surgical department provided. This is a process of searching for something unseen.

Philosophically, epistemology refers to the investigation of the emotional component of representation. It is similar to the process of identifying a disease.

Hume referred to anything that arises in the human mind and becomes the focus of mental activity as a representation. Representations are divided into impressions and ideas. For example, an impression is similar to a good feeling when being under the sun, and an idea is similar to the good feeling when recalling a memory.

The distinction between an impression and an idea is the difference in intensity: an impression is a representation that has a strong force and is usually a feeling or emotion when it first appears in the human mind. Therefore, a doctor's impression of a patient is important, like a compass to find the right path. When a patient has shortness of breath, and the first physician they see does not have medical knowledge that includes idiopathic pulmonary fibrosis characterized by shortness of breath, the impression is not connected to idiopathic pulmonary fibrosis. This cannot lead to a correct diagnosis, and the disease will not be treated.

Acute exacerbation of pulmonary fibrosis is a serious condition with a 60% fatality rate. The most important thing is to suspect an acute exacerbation of pulmonary fibrosis for early diagnosis and treatment. However, patients cannot suspect a disease. If their doctor does not suspect the condition, the patient is at risk of losing their life.

Low-dose chest CT findings of acute exacerbation.

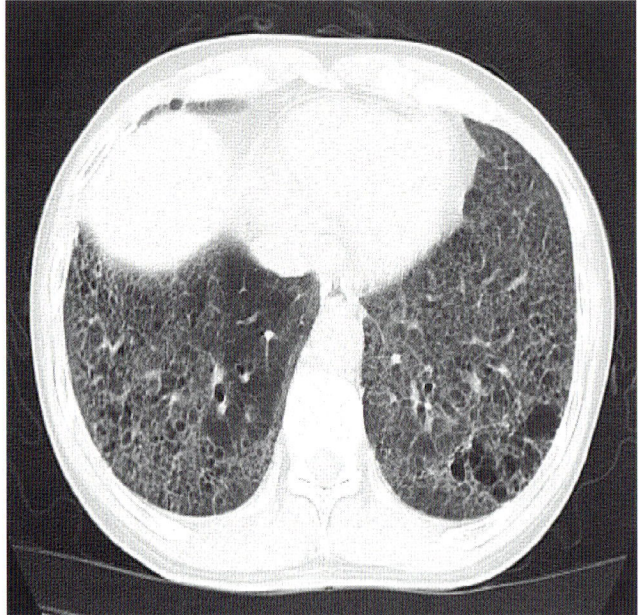

LDCT findings in acute exacerbation of pulmonary fibrosis: honeycombing in both lungs.

Important concepts of acute exacerbation

An acute exacerbation of pulmonary fibrosis is a **very serious condition with a 60% mortality rate.**

Early diagnosis and treatment are critical.
Treatment includes systemic high-dose steroids.

A serious condition with a 60% mortality rate if not treated immediately.

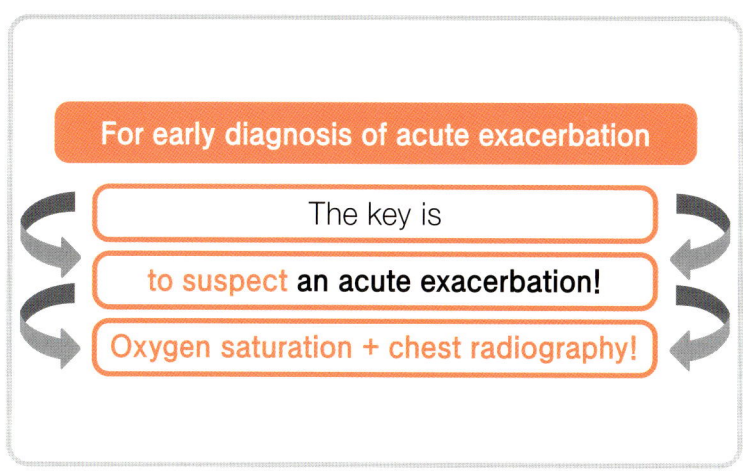

For early diagnosis of acute exacerbation.

Summary of pulmonary fibrosis

1. Diagnosis made with **low-dose or high-resolution CT scans**
2. Symptoms of acute exacerbation: **Oxygen saturation** testing required
3. Possible **early fibrosis** even if chest radiograph is **normal**
4. The core of treatment is **antifibrotic medication (Pirespa®)**
5. **Liver and kidney** function tests required prior to treatment
6. Adverse events associated with medication must be controlled by a specialist

Summary of pulmonary fibrosis.

A doctor who saves a patient's life is a true doctor. The fundamental value of doctors and hospitals is the diagnosis and treatment of human diseases and saving lives.

Cosmetic doctors are important, but they do not regularly deal with life-threatening situations, That heart surgery is more important than upper blepharoplasty, or that lung cancer surgery is more important than orthodontics is not even worth arguing.

Essential healthcare is directly associated with people's lives.

This is why having doctors who cover essential healthcare is vital. It is the value of the profession of medicine. After 30 years of practicing and advocating for essential healthcare, I am deeply concerned about the future of patients with respiratory disease in our country.

02
Characteristics of fatal pneumonia and pneumonia in older adults

Pneumonia is a disease that is familiar to most people. Pneumonia is an inflammation of the lungs with many different medical classifications; however, this book is not about common pneumonia.

Depending on the cause, pneumonia is categorized into bacterial pneumonia, which is caused by bacteria; viral pneumonia, which is caused by a virus; eosinophilic pneumonia, which is specifically caused by an allergic reaction; and interstitial pneumonia, which is caused by certain medications.

The pathogenesis of pneumonia begins when a causative agent enters the lungs, compromising the respiratory system's defenses. This triggers an inflammatory response, leading to lung inflammation as inflammatory cells increase in the body. This type of pneumonia was only in the top 10 of the leading causes of death 30 years ago, but has recently risen to be the third leading cause of death overall.

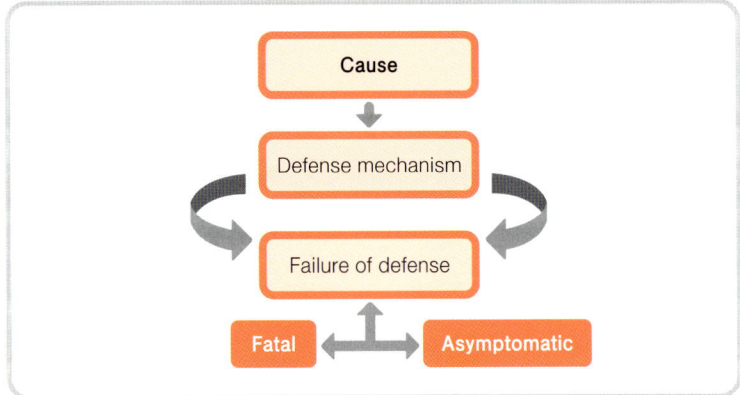

Pathogenesis of pneumonia.

The primary reason for the increase in pneumonia as the cause of death is the growing older adult population. Senile pneumonia may not present with the typical clinical symptoms of pneumonia. Therefore, recognizing the characteristics of senile and fatal pneumonia is important. In particular, acute senile pneumonia, a deadly form of pneumonia, can take a life in a single day.

For older adults with underlying medical conditions, the outcome depends on how quickly pneumonia is diagnosed and treated. Pneumonia is most often accompanied by fever, cough, and sputum. Pneumonia in young people is characterized by very serious symptoms. However, noting the characteristics of senile pneumonia is important because it may not cause fever; patients may not even have a cough. Here are seven characteristics of senile pneumonia:
1) No cough
2) Normal body temperature
3) Generalized weakness
4) No appetite
5) Chest tightness
6) Dizziness
7) Indigestion and hiccups

> **Viral pneumonia**
> **Pneumonia in people with chronic respiratory conditions**
>
> [Increased respiratory rate
>   Increased white blood cells
>   Increased heart rate
>   Decreased blood pressure and consciousness]

Characteristics of fatal pneumonia.

Some readers likely have different opinions on this. The seventh characteristic may be the most outrageous one of all. Hiccups? Pneumonia with no fever or cough but with hiccups?
However, this is true; hiccups can be one of the many symptoms of pneumonia.

Inflammation in the lungs can irritate the diaphragm and cause hiccups. It is almost impossible for a patient to recognize these symptoms as pneumonia.
We live in an age of information overload, and misinformation can be damaging. Consequently, choosing the right information from appropriate sources is important.

Risk factors for developing deadly pneumonia can be summarized as follows:
1) Bronchial asthma
2) Chronic obstructive pulmonary disease (COPD)
3) Bronchiectasis
4) Pulmonary fibrosis
5) Diabetes
6) Heart failure
7) Renal failure

8) Cancer
9) Use of immunosuppressive medications
10) Aged 70 years or older

Among these risk factors for fatal pneumonia, the first four are particularly dangerous. This means that pneumonia with pre-existing lung disease has the potential to become fatal. What are the symptoms of fatal pneumonia?

The most important symptom to look out for in fatal pneumonia is the absence of a fever or a drop in temperature. Pneumonia should not be ruled out in the absence of a fever.

Another characteristic of fatal pneumonia is altered consciousness. Notably, as the lungs are the anatomical organ responsible for human breathing, pneumonia can cause altered consciousness. Altered consciousness can be mistaken for a psychiatric problem. Patients may say strange things, similar to someone with dementia. Fatal pneumonia can also cause a drop in blood pressure. How do patients with pneumonia reach the hospital?

Patients visit the hospital when they have symptoms. However, they may also visit the hospital for a health checkup with no symptoms. Not everyone with a disease has symptoms. Hypertension has no symptoms in the early stages. Patients with hypertension discover they have high blood pressure accidentally when they take a blood pressure reading. Diabetes is also asymptomatic in the early stages. As diabetes progresses, symptoms include dry mouth, weight loss, and frequent urination. Hypercholesterolemia is also asymptomatic but can lead to cardiovascular or cerebrovascular disease if left untreated. There is a risk that a disease can progress and be diagnosed even if there are no symptoms, but when symptoms mimic those of other conditions, a misdiagnosis can put patients at risk. Hospitalization criteria for pneumonia are based on the so-called "CURB" criteria: C for consciousness, U for urea, R for respiration, and B for blood pressure. Thus, if there is a decrease in consciousness, deterioration in kidney function, rapid respiratory rate, and a drop in blood pressure, hospitalization is usually required.

Pneumonia is a very common and potentially dangerous disease that can affect anyone at any age, from newborns and infants to older adults. It is a condition that humans cannot avoid.

03
Is Seoul National University Hospital the best option?

Lung cancer is the number one killer among many cancers. What makes lung cancer a cancer with a high mortality rate? There are three reasons. The first reason is that early diagnosis of lung cancer is very difficult. The second reason lies in the molecular biology of lung cancer itself. The third reason is that it is difficult to cure.

Why is early detection of lung cancer so difficult? A simple chest radiograph will not detect a tumor. Blood tests such as "Cyfra21-1," a tumor marker test, are also limited in their ability to detect lung cancer early. A "smear" test may be performed on patients' sputum, but this is also limited in early detection abilities.

With more than 40 years of efforts by doctors to improve the early detection of lung cancer, low-dose chest CT scanning was found to have clinical significance in early detection of lung cancer and has been accepted as the gold standard by the medical community. Currently, low-dose chest CT scanning is used for early diagnosis of suspected lung cancer, followed by biopsy for confirmation.

Lung cancer is divided into small cell and non-small cell carcinoma based on histologic morphology. Non-small cell carcinoma is further categorized into adenocarcinoma, squamous cell carcinoma, and large cell carcinoma.

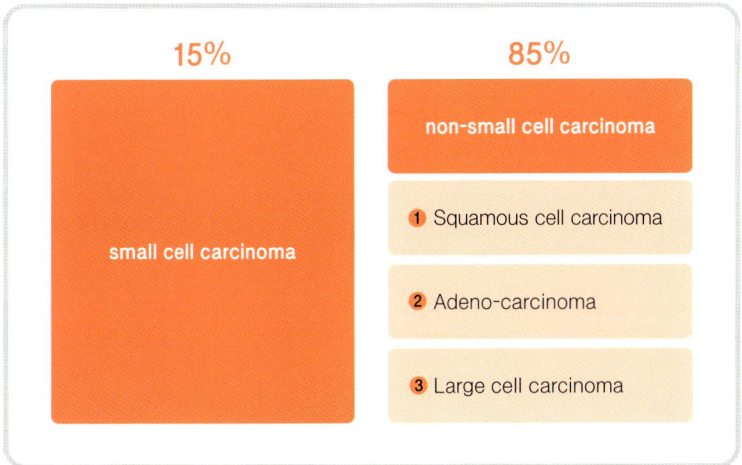

Classification of lung cancer.

Small cell carcinoma is a very specific type of lung cancer. The staging of small cell lung cancer is classified as either limited disease (LD; when the cancer cells are confined to one side of the lung) or extensive disease (ED; when the cancer cells have spread beyond one side of the lung). Some of the important characteristics of small cell carcinoma are as follows:
1) Difficult to diagnosis early
2) Rapid metastasis rate
3) Good response to initial chemotherapy
4) Rapid post-treatment growth of cancer
5) 95% of cases found in smokers
6) The worst of the many forms of lung cancer
7) The most common lung cancer to metastasize to the brain
8) No genetic variants found

Treatment options based on stage include chemotherapy and radiation therapy for LD and chemotherapy for ED.
Readers may think that chemotherapy and radiation would be a good combination for ED because it is a more advanced form of cancer.

However, ED small cell carcinoma cannot be treated with radiation because the cancer cells have already spread throughout the body, making the whole body a target for radiation.

What may surprise readers about the treatment of small cell carcinoma is that, despite remarkable medical advances, the same cancer drugs used 40 years ago are still being used regularly as of today, in April 2024.

The cytotoxic chemotherapy drugs etoposide and cisplatin have been used for four decades. One encouraging fact, however, is that an immunotherapy drug called "Ticentric" has been developed and is currently being used in treatment.

1. Etoposide
2. Cisplatin
3. Ticentric(immunotherapy)

Three standard treatments for small cell lung carcinoma in 2024.

Immune cells help the T cells in the body to fight cancer. Cancer cells evade attacks from T cells by engaging in "immune evasion" against natural anti-cancer T cells.

Immunotherapy is a breakthrough cancer treatment that works by preventing cancer cells from evading T cells, allowing the T cells to kill the cancer cells.

> Activating
> **T cells** in the body

What is immunotherapy?

> Cancer cells carry **mutated genetic antigens**.
> (**T cells attack** the mutated antigens of these cancer cells)
>
> To impede the attack of T cells, cancer cells
> express immune checkpoint protein (PDL-1).
>
> **Immunotherapy** binds to the PDL-1 expressed
> by cancer cells and enables the body's own multicellular
> immune system to attack cancer.

Interactions between T cells and cancer cells.

I saw a male patient who had been smoking for 45 years. He had been treated for bronchial asthma and COPD at local and semi-general hospitals for breathing difficulties and had been coughing up sputum for five years. He presented at our clinic because his symptoms had intensified over the past six months. He was a heavy smoker with pre-existing COPD.

Doctors should question the validity of a diagnosis and treatment when a patient's symptoms do not disappear or worsen clinically while receiving treatment.

"I think, therefore I am (cogito, ergo sum)," is a famous saying from the French philosopher René Descartes. These words, conveying the principle of his philosophy, were introduced in 1641, about 383 years ago, laying the groundwork for modern philosophy.

This principle is the starting point of philosophy, a proposition expressing one's self-certainty that, although one can doubt everything and think unity is false, one cannot doubt the existence of human beings who doubt and think as such.

In response to the statement "I think," the statement "therefore I am" expresses what is intuitively grasped.

Medicine is a domain of the natural sciences, yet also closely related to the humanities. When seeking a scientific basis and evidence, the cause is found and objectively analyzed and treated, and the treatment is quantified to reach statistical significance; doctors call this a standard diagnostic method and treatment. Doctors apply these rules to examine and treat patients; however, a critical error can exist in this.

Potentially, despite the physician's belief that the initial diagnosis is based on objective fact or scientific evidence, new variables could emerge during the course of the treatment. At this juncture, the patient's condition is critical, and the doctor faces a challenge. This is when the doctor should suspect other causes.

Suspicious doctors save patients; unsuspicious doctors lose them.

Therefore, a doctor exists to check, doubt, and think about the overall diagnosis of a disease, course of treatment, and response of the patient.

Healthcare should be philosophical and humanistic because it deals with people. In the case of the aforementioned male patient, the diagnosis was correct, as was the treatment provided based on for that diagnosis; however, they overlooked the fact that the patient was at high risk for developing other serious conditions. Patients with COPD are at high risk for developing lung cancer. Smoking itself is also a risk factor for lung cancer.

Given his age, smoking habits, COPD, and symptoms that worsened with treatment, this patient's risk for developing lung cancer should have been recognized and suspected. Simple chest radiographs or pulmonary function tests are insufficient for diagnosing lung cancer. An accurate diagnosis requires a chest CT and bronchoscopy with biopsy. The patient was diagnosed with ED small cell carcinoma, which is known for having the worst prognosis among the different types of lung cancer. A diagnosis shall be followed by treatment, and for ED, he had to be treated with chemo injections.

What makes a good doctor? What type of doctors are so-called "good doctors"?

I diagnosed this patient very quickly and accurately and told him he needed chemotherapy. The patient and his guardian requested me to fill out a referral form for admission to Seoul National University Hospital.
The patient's home was in Busan, South Korea. I checked with the oncology department at Seoul National University Hospital for an appointment. The first available appointment was three months later. I spoke to the patient and guardian again, explaining it was not important to choose a famous hospital in Seoul but to choose the one where he could receive chemo injections the soonest. I also explained in detail why.
I tried to convince him that the chemotherapy treatment at Seoul National University Hospital was identical to that at other hospitals like Pusan National University Hospital, Paik Hospital, Dong-A University Hospital, and Kosin University Gospel Hospital in Busan. With the same treatment, the efficacy is the same. I insisted that waiting three months for treatment at a prestigious hospital was a foolish choice that would extinguish the remaining embers of his life.
Patients do not know. They have no idea what to do when they are ill.

Sometimes, even doctors have no idea.

Giving patients an accurate diagnosis is not enough to make a good doctor. A good doctor should have insight into the natural course of a disease, what the treatment options are for that disease, and which hospital is the best choice given the patient's circumstances.

This is also the fundamental reason why doctors should be philosophical and humanistic.

04
Sincerity is the way of Heaven

Mencius said, "Sincerity is the way of Heaven."

This proverb, which suggests that even the heavens are touched by the utmost sincerity, conveys the idea that no matter how impossible a task is, it will eventually be accomplished if one has the will and conviction to persevere.

Similar English sayings include "Heaven helps those who help themselves" and "Where there's a will, there's a way."

In February 2024, I was having a very busy day at work. When the clinic opens at 7:30 a.m., it feels like stepping onto a battlefield. I barely have time to even use the bathroom. In addition to the scheduled critical and respiratory patients, many patients show up without an appointment.

The Beautiful Breath Clinic is classified as a primary healthcare institution in the healthcare delivery system. Simply, the clinic is a private practice in a neighborhood. However, it is not just the locals who visit the clinic. Patients come from all over South Korea.
Although high-speed trains travel between here and both Busan and Mokpo, the popularity of my clinic still makes me feel surprised and grateful.

Patients fly from Jeju Island, travel by ferry from Ulleungdo to Pohang and take a long drive from there, and come here from Wando. Patients come from all over the country: Haenam, the town at the end of the Korean peninsula, Gangwon-do, Chungcheong-do, Gyeongsangbuk-do, Gyeongsangbuk-do, Gyeongsangnam-do, Jeollabuk-do, Jeollanam-do, Jeollanam-do, Sejong-si, and Daejeon-si.

As I wrapped up my day around 4 p.m., I spoke on the phone with a professor who works at the lung cancer center of one of the big five hospitals in South Korea. He said he had been trying to talk to me for a month and had been unable to reach me. Our phone conversation was brief and simple.

A patient who underwent a bronchoscopic biopsy at the Beautiful Breath Clinic had gone to the lung cancer center for chemotherapy. The faculty members at the university hospital's cancer center wondered how a bronchoscopic biopsy could be performed at a private practice clinic; however, after seeing the results of the biopsy, they reached out to me.

In addition to providing words of encouragement and expressing his curiosity, he suggested creating a collaborative hospital relationship in which patients with suspected lung cancer at the university hospital could be referred to the Beautiful Breath Clinic for bronchoscopic biopsies.

The above may not mean much to readers who are not doctors. However, doctors would find it hard to believe. A university hospital operating one of the five largest lung cancer centers in South Korea referring a lung cancer patient to the Beautiful Breath Clinic, a humble private practice in Anam-dong, Seongbuk-gu, for a biopsy? Making such a referral was possible for a gastroscopy or colonoscopy; however, to do so for a bronchoscopy was unprecedented in the history of medicine in South Korea.

Knowing the size of the university hospital, I was very concerned. I knew there would be a wide variety of lung cancer patients, and that this would include many difficult and critical patients. I told him I would do my best.

The patients coming from the university hospital often presented with a challenging set of conditions. The most important thing to keep in mind for bronchoscopic biopsy of lung cancer is the anatomic location of the tumor. Patients with tumors in easier anatomical locations were taking medications that could cause bleeding, had experienced a stroke, or had a heart condition, while those without underlying medical conditions had tumors in very difficult locations.

Bronchoscopy in patients with severe bronchiectasis is difficult enough, but it becomes even more so in patients with lung cancer, as this requires taking substantial tissue samples for referral to a professor of anatomical pathology.

Why is having thorough biopsies so important?

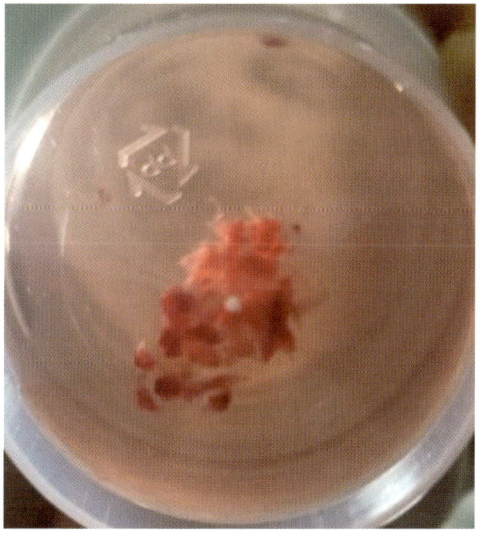

Photograph of more than 20 pieces of tissue removed from a lung tumor.

In addition to the different forms of lung cancer, testing for genetic mutations is needed to identify critical reference points when selecting anti-cancer drugs for chemotherapy. Among the most well-known and treatable genetic mutations is to a gene called the epidermal growth factor receptor (EGFR). The EGFR gene mutation is a unique and only seen in lung cancer.

Targeted anti-cancer drugs work very well with EGFR. Unlike cytotoxic anticancer drugs, targeted anti-cancer drugs target the genes of cancer cells and kill only cancer cells, resulting in fewer adverse events and superior treatment effects.

These targeted agents range from the first through the fourth generation and are used to treat cancer. Lexarza, a third-generation targeted anti-cancer drug developed by a South Korean pharmaceutical company called Yuhan Corporation, demonstrates excellent therapeutic effects comparable to those of foreign third-generation targeted anti-cancer drugs.

Since I opened my practice as SEONGLIM JIN Clinic 23 years ago, and through changing the name to the Beautiful Breath Clinic 19 years ago, I have focused on treating respiratory diseases.

When I announced in 2006 that I would be performing bronchoscopy in a private practice for the first time in South Korea, other doctors were skeptical. Patients may not realize how laborious and technically demanding this test is, with the burden of providing emergency care in the event of complications. However, doctors do, which is why they did not believe it at first. The saying "sincerity is the way of Heaven" really resonates with me.

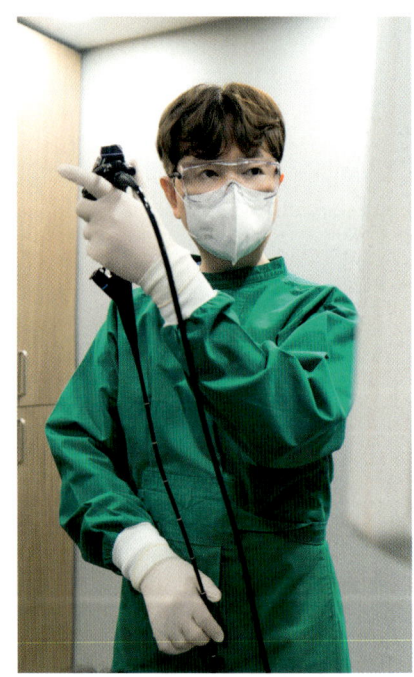

Dr. SEONGLIM JIN performing a bronchoscopy.

Performing bronchoscopies has been rewarding and joyful, giving me a sense of pride, but it has also been incredibly stressful.

It has taken a lot of hard work for me, along with the Beautiful Breath Clinic staff over the last 19 years, to remain a place where a university hospital with the best lung cancer center in South Korea and the largest in Asia recognizes the accuracy, speed, and reliability of our bronchoscopy.

For this honor, I believe I am indebted to my staff, who have prepared me well for my bronchoscopy, helped me through extreme tension every day, and fulfilled their duties in an orderly manner in the event of an emergency.

I am who I am today thanks to the brilliant minds at the Beautiful Breath Clinic.

05
Diagnoses lie in the words of patients

What will be the most important thing for doctors to know when treating symptomatic patients in 2024?
Is it a CT scan, MRI, ultrasound, or endoscopy finding? It may come as a surprise, but the most fundamental and important aspect of diagnosis in internal medicine—the branch of medicine that treats illness with drugs and injections, not surgery, and whose job it is to identify diagnoses that require surgery and refer them appropriately—is the word of the patient.
When patients describe a wide range of symptoms, the doctor's job is to select carefully those that are relevant to the patient's current condition to reach the core symptoms. When shortness of breath is the most common current clinical symptom, the patient may begin talking about indigestion. Some patients report coughing when chest pain as their most important symptom at the moment.
In short, patients are not medically trained and, moreover, have no experience in helping others with medical knowledge. Therefore, they provide their doctors with a comprehensive account of all their symptoms. In the age of the Internet, we are inundated with information—some of which is beneficial, some of which is not, and some of which may even be harmful. In this flood of information, wise consumers are able to separate the truth from the lies.
The same is true when a doctor listens to a patient's symptoms. Since patients do not know exactly what their condition is, they list their symptoms and discomforts without elaboration. They may say their stomach hurts, then their chest hurts, complain of shortness of breath, then move on to chest pain. When talking about a headache, they

may also complain of coughing up sputum and then mention a stiff back. Doctors can get confused listening to patient's words without interruptions.

When a doctor meets a patient for the first time, the first piece of information to uncover is why the patient has come to see the doctor. It would be rare for people to visit a physician in anger after an argument with their spouse. No patient would visit an internal medicine clinic because they feel upset after a fight with a friend.

In other words, over 90% of patients who visit a physician actually feel physically sick in some way. They need a physician to sort it out for them. How well a physician can untangle the jumble depends on his or her competence.

The key is to identify the most important symptom, which doctors call the "chief complaint." Identifying the chief complaint is critical, as it provides the basis for treating the patient. Depending on a patient's chief complaint, the diagnosis can be categorized into a respiratory, cardiac, digestive, endocrine, or renal disease.

A 74-year-old female patient presented with chest pain. This patient had visited the clinic in 2001, the year it opened, and has since built a strong rapport with me. A high level of doctor-patient rapport is an invaluable asset when providing medical care.

She complained of chest pain and the sensation of a foreign body and pain in her bronchial area. Chest pain and bronchial foreign body sensation can be seen in a number of respiratory conditions; however, most of them are accompanied by coughing and shortness of breath, while chest pain and bronchial foreign body sensation alone is less common. I asked more detailed questions to narrow down the possibilities. These questions were intended to sort out unnecessary information and identify the chief complaint. Simply asking detailed questions does not do any good.

The reason a doctor asks these detailed questions is to rule out unrelated conditions and eventually find the root cause of the current symptoms. When a patient complains of chest pain, the attending doctor should consider two types of emergencies.

Specifically, the doctor should check for cardiovascular emergencies first and respiratory emergencies second. Although the patient is bound for further examination, the doctor can already tell if there is an emergency by listening for symptoms of chest pain.

Doctors often recognize emergency chest pain by the look on the patients' face, providing immediate clarity regarding the situation. Chest pain in heart disease tends to come and go, but chest pain during a heart attack is not just any pain. It is a sharp ache that feels like one's chest is about to explode. Symptoms other than chest pain are also evident. The patient breaks out in a cold sweat, becomes disoriented, and hunches over due to the overwhelming pain. Chest pain in a respiratory emergency is accompanied by frequent shortness of breath and coughing, and it is generalized rather than localized or only occurring when the patient breathes deeply.

This particular patient was not experiencing the chest pain of an emergency cardiovascular or respiratory event. However, the most basic EKG and chest X-ray still needed to be performed. Both tests came back normal. I sighed and started questioning the patient again. When I was asking questions about the situation when the chest pain first occurred, the patient said in passing, "I think the chest pain started after I had the fish soup." The patient did not seem to put much weight on it, but I thought this was it. I thought I knew what was causing her symptoms.

My staff looked at me with bewilderment as I told them to prepare for a gastroscopy and to bring forceps, instruments used for biopsies (medical devices with a long wire on the end and small pincers used to examine tissue).

It was not long into the gastroscopy that the puzzled looks on the faces of the staff members turned to a "wow!" I performed a gastroscopy to get a closer look at the patient's throat and tonsils. They were clean. However, upon entering the esophageal region, I spotted a foreign body lodged across the lining of the upper esophagus. It was not just hanging; it was stuck. It had long, pointed ends lodged into both sides of the patient's upper esophagus. I needed to remove this unidentified foreign body myself, as the university hospitals were dysfunctional at the time due to the resignations of residents.

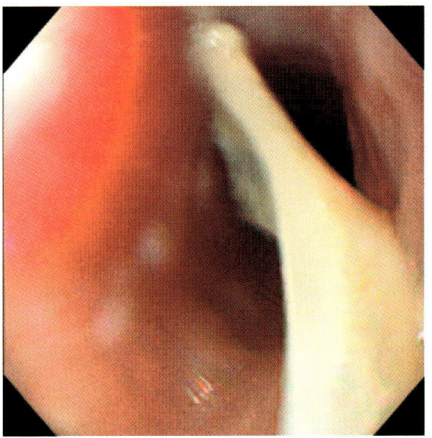

Gastroscopy: Fish bone stuck in the upper esophagus; lodged in the esophageal mucosa causing a dangerous situation.

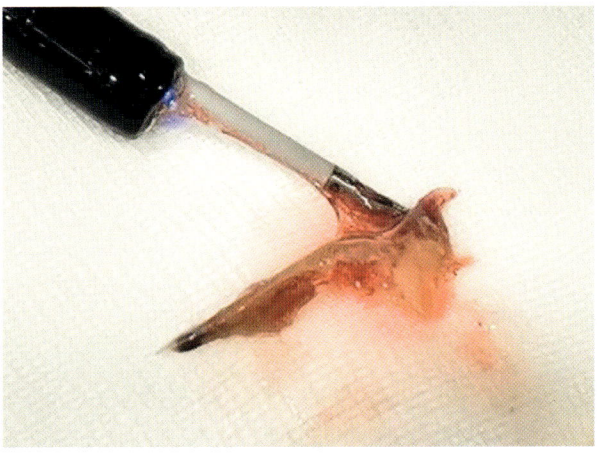

Photograph of a sharp fish bone removed using endoscopic biopsy forceps.

As a pulmonologist, I am better and more confident in performing bronchoscopies than gastroscopies. Removing a foreign body from the bronchi is an incredibly difficult and risky procedure that requires the top-notch skills recognized by endoscopists.

I mentioned in my previous book that I once used bronchoscopy to remove three dentures lodged in a patient's bronchi. An elderly patient had been to three university hospitals and several "private practices" for chest pain over a period of more than six months. This patient was only tested for cardiovascular systems and given medication after being misdiagnosed with heart disease. I performed a bronchoscopy to remove a very large monkfish bone lodged in this patient's left upper lobe bronchus.

This time, I had to remove an unidentified foreign body lodged in a patient's esophagus—specifically, in the upper esophagus with thin esophageal mucosa. I have seen the oddest patients; however, this was something that should have been handled by the department of gastroenterology. The patient, however, had not received the treatment she needed in time due to the healthcare delivery of university hospitals being downsized following the resignations of residents. If not removed immediately, the foreign body in the esophagus could lead to esophageal rupture, which could be life-threatening.

The procedure to remove a foreign body from the esophagus is not a simple one. The mucous membrane of the esophagus is very thin, and even a small cut can cause esophageal rupture, which is a serious condition that requires surgery. After carefully grasping the foreign object with forceps, I successfully removed it. Upon identifying the foreign body, I was surprised, as was everyone in the endoscopy room. The fishbone was very sharp at both ends. Those sharp ends had been lodged in the mucous membranes on both sides of the esophagus. It was frightening. Although the patient was at a higher risk of esophageal rupture, the fishbone was removed well.

I learned a big lesson.

I learned a big lesson from this. It reminded me of how important it is to listen carefully to how patients describe their symptoms, followed by quick thinking and quick action. For this, doctors need to stay sharp and skilled.

More importantly, when faced with a patient's symptoms, it is important to have good knowledge of the medical condition with which the patient is presenting, as well as a wide scope of medical knowledge that allows for consideration of not only emergencies but various clinical situations.
It also requires having the courage and skill to go through with a procedure when feeling confident about a suspected condition.
Doctors are essential to our society. Should doctors not live up to their worth as essential beings, with no shame to their names?

Chapter 3

Watch out for kind doctors

———

A country where helping a poor patient is a crime

———

On the importance of discernment

———

The quintessential preaching to deaf ears

———

The paradox of prognosis

———

The truth and lies of HIRA healthcare quality assessment

01
Watch out for kind doctors

The dictionary defines being "kind" as behaving very cordially and courteously, with synonyms including amiable, gentle, and "sweetfriendly" (soft and sweet). No one dislikes kindness, and people who are friendly are well-liked by those around them.

There is a Korean proverb, "Kind sympathy enters through iron doors." The proverb suggests that a genuine caring heart will come through, even to the bluntest of people. Kindness and unkindness immediately present good and bad images of ourselves to others.

After 30 years of practicing medicine, why am I saying this strange thing about being wary of kind doctors?

Taking it one step further—is a kind doctor always the right doctor? Is a kind professor always a good professor? Although this question may sound philosophical question, it is indeed practical.

What type of doctor do you want to go to when you are sick? Would you go to a doctor who is kind but not as skilled in the specialty, or would you rather go to a doctor who is not kind but has the best skills in the specialty? This may seem like a silly question, but people often find themselves in this situation.

As a pulmonologist dedicated to diagnosing and treating respiratory diseases, I have experienced my fair share of the kind doctor error. Kindness is a valuable virtue that everyone should have and a quality that is important to life and shows a lot about someone's character.

However, for doctors who are diagnosing and treating patients, kindness can be nothing more than a formality. A good doctor is always right. Doctors should always strive to be the best in their specialty, particularly those who specialize in essential healthcare practices. Kindness does not save lives. Skills do.

A good and kind doctor deserves to be called the best. What I am emphasizing here is a side effect of the "service ethos" that first infiltrated the healthcare industry 20 years ago.

I believe that adopting a customer-centered service ethos is a positive change in healthcare. The introduction of a patient-centered service ethos into the hospital system, which was once a symbol of authoritarianism, is a salutary phenomenon that fits the zeitgeist. However, this phenomenon has led to some hospitals and doctors developing false perceptions and to patients having some serious misconceptions.

Determining which doctors are skillful is difficult for patients. The nature of medicine does not allow non-medical patients to judge a doctor's skills. Therefore, patients often favor kind doctors and assume they are also good doctors and have the best skills. However, some bad doctors take advantage of such misunderstandings in patients. Some bad doctors take advantage of patients commercially under the guise of kindness. This can have even more serious consequences, such as a delayed diagnosis because of a lack of skills. However, a delayed diagnosis may not be the worst of the patient's problems.

An incorrect diagnosis leads to incorrect treatment. Obviously, patients' health and lives are placed in jeopardy, and in some cases, even lost. This does not occur only with critically ill patients.

Many patients who go to the doctor for a minor cold or body ache end up with serious adverse events caused by medications. All medications are associated with adverse events, with no medications being absolutely free from them. When prescribing medication, a good doctor should be familiar with its efficacy as well as the possible adverse events. This means that doctors should be aware that some medications may not be prescribed to children under 12 years of age, while others may require caution when prescribed to older adults.

Doctors should have full medical knowledge of the interactions between medications and consider all possibilities, such as cases with poor liver function, kidney disease, or concomitant medications.

There was a 31-year-old female patient with a job related to cosmetology. She went to a local doctor for a sore throat and was prescribed medication. She went to the local clinic for two reasons, one of which was that the doctor was very kind. In my 30 years as a physician, this was the first time I heard of a doctor performing an intravenous (IV) infusion himself on a patient. This doctor was not an essential healthcare specialist.

Essential healthcare providers do not administer peripheral vascular or nutritional fluids themselves. Nutrition and fluids are given by a nurse or nursing assistant. Injections administered directly by a doctor are injections of chemotherapy drugs.

Peripheral vascular procedures are the job of nurses, whereas doctors perform more difficult procedures such as central venous procedures and arterial blood tests. If a doctor in that hospital wants to give an IV infusion himself, he is free to do so, and should not be criticized. However, if the doctor has an ulterior motive for the procedure, it becomes reprehensible behavior.

The patient's other reason was that the doctor had a reputation for helping people get better quickly. She presented with generalized weakness, difficulty breathing, and facial swelling. As many patients who come to the clinic have been treated elsewhere, it is important to check their medications. I checked the patient's prescription and was very surprised to see a medication that was not meant for treating a 31-year-old patient's sore throat.

This patient was prescribed an ultra-potent steroid drug called methylprednisolone, and while this is a very important drug, it should not be prescribed for a simple sore throat. Methylprednisolone is an ultra-potent steroid I occasionally prescribe as a pulmonologist for respiratory emergencies. Prescribing such an ultra-potent steroid associated with significant adverse events for a common cold or simple sore throat can only mean it is being used to relieve the patient's symptoms instantly.

Such a prescription can cause potentially life-threatening adverse events, some of which may result in irreversible damage. You may not think this is a serious situation because it is not life-threatening; however, for this patient, it is just as important as if it were.

I have encountered countless cases like this one. I could provide too many examples of doctors prescribing steroid inhalers to patients with bronchial tuberculosis for more than a year, prescribing antibiotics to patients with hypersensitivity pneumonitis for a long time without prescribing steroids, not testing patients with stage IV lung cancer for gene mutations while performing biopsies, prescribing anti-inflammatory drugs to patients with fungal infections and making their illness worse, and prescribing medications to help patients with bronchiectasis to clear their sputum while saying antibiotics are dangerous.

While it is unacceptable for some doctors to engage in such behavior unknowingly, it is even more troubling when they do so deliberately. Surprisingly, these doctors have one thing in common. The thing is, not a single one of these doctors appears to be "unkind."

Doctors are not entertainers.

Hospitals are not big agencies. A doctor's fundamental function is to treat patients, while that of a hospital is to provide good equipment and systems. While unkind doctors are not desirable, nice quack doctors are really bad doctors.

What is the most important virtue for a good doctor?

A good doctor is one who can save lives, and skills not kindness can save patients. The reason why all essential healthcare doctors need to be at the top of their game is because they are handling the lives of their patients.

Working backwards, really good doctors simply have a kind personality that shines through. They do not purposefully overstate their kindness to show a friendly demeanor. Therefore, dear readers, be wary of doctors who emphasize nothing but extraordinary kindness!

Still waters run deep. Good doctors who care about their patients never make a fuss.

True kindness comes in an understated and refined form.

02
A country where helping a poor patient is a crime

According to its dictionary meaning, the word "poor" is an adjective that describes the state of being in mental and physical distress because one lacks sufficient means of subsistence. Synonyms for poor include needy and desperate.

However, the dictionary meaning does not necessarily tell the truth. Many people have a lot of money but are in a state of distress, while many others are comfortable and carefree but in a state of physical discomfort.

In this book, "poor" describes a category of people who are sick but cannot afford to go to the doctor. Helping the poor is a beautiful thing and a good deed that reveals the good heart of human beings, whether in the East or the West or ancient or modern times. Without going into a long-winded explanation, this is something we all instinctively feel.

What about picking on the poor? Picking on people is a bad thing, and those who do it are considered bullies. Laws exist against harassing people. Even without considering legal relationships, our emotions tell us that bullying others is a terrible thing that should not be done.

Although most readers will be unaware, I would like to tell you something about the South Korean healthcare system that is practiced openly. I want every citizen and politician in our country to realize that this unethical and ridiculous system that defies common sense is being implemented, and I hope this flawed system will be fixed as soon as possible.

Before I tell this patient's story, I must tell the readers something about the health insurance system that they need to know and understand.

Health insurance is a form of medical coverage, which is a social security system where the government uses public funds to pay for medical expenses (diagnosis and treatment) on behalf of patients who cannot afford it so they do not have to pay for medical services.

To keep the poor healthy, money is provided for essential or basic medical conditions. Areas such as cosmetology, bariatrics, and plastic surgery are not supported. In more technical terms, the concept of healthcare that is connected to a person's life is called "fundamental rights" healthcare, while the opposite concept is called "commodity" healthcare. Examples of "commodity" healthcare include plastic surgery, teeth whitening, obesity treatment, and orthodontics. However, some "fundamental rights" healthcare services are not covered by insurance. The most common example is the "sleep management fee" for procedures such as gastroscopy, colonoscopy, and bronchoscopy.

The typical medication used during sleep endoscopy, an injection of midazolam, is covered by health insurance; however, the additional costs called "sleep management costs," including the labor cost of extra staff and costs of occupying the bed and caring for the patient while asleep, are not legally covered.

"Non-covered" is the opposite of "covered," meaning that it is not covered by the national insurance fund and paid entirely out of pocket. South Korea categorizes poor patients into two types of Medicaid beneficiaries to help with their medical expenses. Patients must meet at least one of three criteria to qualify as Type 1 Medicaid beneficiaries.

First, one has to be a basic livelihood security recipient. Basic livelihood security recipients are people who are incapable of working (under 18/65+), registered with a serious illness such as cancer or severe burns, registered with one of 107 rare and incurable diseases, or institutionalized.

Second, one has to be a homeless patient. Homeless patients do not have a fixed place of residence or are been brought to the hospital by local administrative authorities, and those who do not have a caretaker or, if they do, that person is either unwilling or unable to provide care. Third, one has to be covered by other laws, including refugees, injured patriots, families of deceased patriots, adopted children under the age of 18, national heroes, those involved in the May 18 Uprising, North Korean defectors, successors of important intangible cultural properties, and the homeless.

Type 2 Medicaid beneficiaries are those who are eligible for basic livelihood security but not Type 1 Medicaid benefits. In addition to the medical protection system, another system pays medical expenses for those categorized as part of the "disadvantaged group."

The criteria for who are considered part of a "disadvantaged group" are those who potentially have low incomes but are ineligible for basic livelihood security because they have fixed assets or dependent household members. They have a median household income of 50% or less, fixed assets, or family members with an income who are obligated to support them.

In April 2024, during a dust storm, a patient come to my office presenting with symptoms of shortness of breath, hemoptysis (blood in sputum), and a chronic cough. The patient is a longtime smoker. Chest radiography, an imaging test, shows a suspected tumor in the lungs, and lung cancer is strongly suspected due to the presence of bloody sputum and a tumor.

Lung cancer cannot be diagnosed by a chest X-ray or CT scan. It can be suspected, but a biopsy of the tumor is needed to confirm the diagnosis. In this patient, the tumor is located in the central part of the lung and requires bronchoscopy for biopsy.

This is where the ridiculous Medical Service Act of South Korea really comes into play. Among the various endoscopic procedures available, bronchoscopy is often considered the most painful for patients. Thirty years ago, no medications were available for sleep endoscopy, despite the pain associated with this procedure.

Think about it: Even a small amount of water entering the airway causes severe coughing and pain. Furthermore, the instruments used to perform bronchoscopy 30 years ago were much thicker than those we have today. In short, it felt like a metal pipe going directly into your airway. Moreover, it is not performed just look at the airway but to scour every nook and cranny of the bronchi.

Bronchoscopic biopsies take longer and are naturally more painful compared to other similar procedures. Narcotic pain medications are not used for gastroscopies or colonoscopies; however, patients undergoing bronchoscopy are given narcotic pain medications before the procedure. Even with premedication with narcotic pain medications, the patient may be in too much pain to proceed with the procedure. The patient remains lucid and the pain feels like their bronchi are tearing. The fear of not being able to breathe is so overwhelming that the patient may become uncontrollably violent.

Although bronchoscopy remains the most painful examination of all, medicine has come a long way over the years. The invention of sleep-inducing drugs and general anesthetics such as midazolam, propofol, and etomidate has enabled sleep endoscopy.

Patients often undergo a gastroscopy or colonoscopy asleep; however, they can undergo a gastroscopy while awake. I once received a non-sleep gastroscopy, and while I was certainly uncomfortable, the procedure was tolerable. A colonoscopy can also be done while the patient asleep and is much more uncomfortable and painful than a gastroscopy.

It would be absurd to have a non-sleep bronchoscopy. Non-sleeping bronchoscopies can be unsuccessful due to a lack of patient cooperation, especially in situations where biopsies are required. Thus, from both the patient and doctor perspectives, performing a sleep bronchoscopy is not only reasonable and safe but also yields more accurate results.

You may now be asking, what is the problem here? Why am I rambling on about this? What does any of this have to do with helping a poor patient constituting a violation of the law?

As I said above, the "sleep management fee" is not covered by the health insurance. It is a 100% out-of-pocket item. When Type 1 Medicaid beneficiaries have a non-sleep bronchoscopy, they do not pay the hospital. You heard it right; it is free of charge. For Type 1 Medicaid beneficiaries, all clinic appointments, tests, and biopsies are free.

Do You Know Bronchoscopy?

Q. What is a bronchoscopy?

A bronchoscopy is a test to check conditions from the larynx to the bronchi, where a scope is inserted through the mouth and into the bronchi to allow direct visualization of the inside of the bronchi.

Q. What is a bronchoscopy for?

This test is performed for accurate diagnosis when a foreign body is lodged in the trachea or bronchi and needs to be removed directly, or when a disease of the throat, trachea, bronchi, or lungs is suspected.

Q. What can we check with bronchoscopy?

- Sputum (for bacteria, antibiotic resistance, tuberculosis bacteria, cancer cells, and abnormal cells)
- Diagnosis and staging of lung cancer
- Diagnosis of pulmonary or bronchial tuberculosis
- Identification of the causative agent of pneumonia
- Identification of the cause, site, and status of hemoptysis
- Identification of airway obstruction
- Diagnosis of chronic cough of unclear etiology
- Diagnosis of bronchiectasis and other airway and pulmonary diseases

At the Beautiful Breath Clinic, a team led by a highly skilled and experienced pulmonologist performs precise examinations using state-of-the-art endoscopic equipment.

Guidance for bronchoscopy.

All expenses are paid by the country. So far, so good. Our country must be a bona fide healthcare consumer paradise. Yes, it is. There is no other country in the world where patients do not pay for bronchoscopies and biopsies. South Korea is truly a paradise for patients.

The same test in the United States would be worth tens of millions of Korean won. If a Type 1 Medicaid beneficiary attempts to have a bronchoscopy painlessly while asleep, they will be responsible for 100% of the non-covered costs of the "sleep management fee." In the scenario described above, the patient had no money and could not afford the extra cost of a sleep bronchoscopy. A bronchoscopy is essential to diagnose lung cancer: for patients to be examined painlessly and accurately, a sleep bronchoscopy is required.

The choice is one of two.

Should we flip a coin and if it comes up heads, sleep and if it comes up tails, non-sleep?

What would you do, readers, if you were in the same situation? What would you do if you were a doctor? Wouldn't the doctor want to help? Wouldn't all doctors want to help? I really did. How about a free sleep bronchoscopy without charging a "sleep management fee?"

This is not even a huge help, but just the natural and right thing to do. The "sleep management fee" does not cost a fortune like it does in the United States, and even if it did, I would have been willing to help. However, if I provide a free sleep bronchoscopy to a Type 1 patient, the Ministry of Health and Welfare will sue me for violating the Medical Service Act. I would be considered a doctor who broke the law and be punished.

What? Am I joking?

No, this is true. The Medical Services Act works that way. As of April 2024, as I am writing this, Article 27(3) of the Medical Services Act prohibits waiving or discounting out-of-pocket expenses.

Why? That is how it is. The current Medical Services Act punishes doctors for helping patients under the provision called "prohibition against luring of patients." The law was originally intended to prevent plastic surgery, dermatology, dentistry, and cancer care hospitals from advertising and offering discounts to lure patients.

However, laws are not flexible once they are set in stone. It does not matter how well-meaning I am or if I plead that I have done the test for free to help a Type 1 Medicaid patient. I would be a doctor who broke the law and subject to administrative penalties.
All men are equal before the law. That is justice. However, how should the law apply to this patient?
The patient in the example above is just the tip of the iceberg. Why are young doctors turning away from essential healthcare? It is not just about the money.
The government only talks about money when money is not the only cause. While they talk about money, they do not properly increase the fee, not even by a quarter of the basic inflation rate. Essential healthcare has no future in our country. In a book I wrote six years ago, I said that essential healthcare had no hope. The only way to resuscitate it is to change the perceptions of the people in our country.
Do you think money can buy true love? The same goes for the minds of doctors who work in essential healthcare. They cannot be bought with money.
What happened to this patient? He received a sleep bronchoscopy that went well and had a good post-operative prognosis. Did the patient pay for it?
That is a secret I cannot tell in this book. If you have an answer in mind, that is it.

03
On the importance of discernment

Discernment is the ability to see and differentiate between things. To be discerning is to have good judgment when looking at a phenomenon, object, or person to distinguish between good and bad. However, it is more than standard for judging good, but an important character trait for leading a decent life.

Discernment is also crucial in medicine. Discernment is judgment by sight and should be the first thing a doctor does when examining a patient. When a doctor examines a patient, he or she may use the following methods: visual observation (observing with the eyes), auscultation (listening to the patient's breathing or heart sounds with a stethoscope), palpation (touching the patient's body with the hands), and percussion (tapping the patient's body with the hands).

This has been an important practice of doctors since ancient times. Recently, scientific and medical advances have somewhat

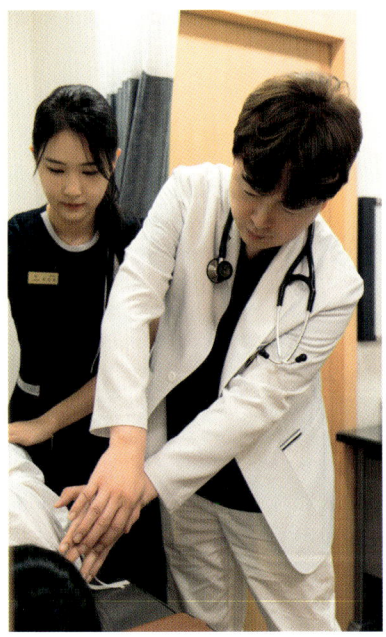

Director SEONGLIM JIN examining whether the pleura is filled with water.

marginalized the physical examination (visual observation, auscultation, palpation, and percussion), but it remains important in the practice of internal medicine.

When we picture a doctor, the image of a stethoscope usually comes to mind. The stethoscope is among the most important tools when seeing a patient in respiratory medicine, as it allows us to listen to the sounds of the patient breathing to speculate on and diagnose various respiratory diseases.

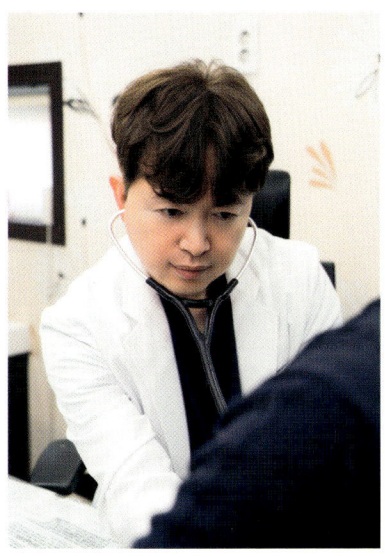

Dr. SEONGLIM JIN using a stethoscope to listen to the breath sounds of patients.

The stethoscope was invented by the French physician René Laennec. There is this story of the invention of the stethoscope involving a busty woman. In 1816, when examining young, plump women complaining of heart pain, doctors had no choice but to put their ears directly to the patient's ample breasts.

Before the invention of the stethoscope, doctors would put their ear directly to a patient's chest to hear the heart or listen for alveolar sounds. Doctors still use this method in emergency situations in which they do not have a stethoscope.

However, when treating younger women, doctors are very cautious and rarely practice this classic method because it can later be misinterpreted as "molestation." Inspired by how children play by tapping one end of a wooden stick against their ears to hear sounds, Laennec rolled up a piece of paper and placed it on the patient's chest, which allowed him to hear the patient's heart more clearly.

This was the world's first stethoscope. The prototype for the modern stethoscope, the one placed in both ears as readers would recognize, was developed in 1843 and used for more than a century before being replaced by the modern stethoscope in the 1970s. The stethoscope remains the most powerful yet simple tool for diagnosing lung disease among many other conditions in internal medicine.

As a pulmonologist, I use a stethoscope to listen to patients' breath sounds over 800 times a day (at least four times on a single patient) and have done so more than two million times to date. How do discerning eyes work in healthcare?

A visual examination is when a doctor looks directly at a patient and notes any external changes to diagnose a disease based on their complexion, eyes, mouth, nose, ears, and tongue. Visual observation is important for diagnosing patients with emergency respiratory diseases.

The wait times for appointments at the Beautiful Breath Clinic are long. Although this is unfortunate, and we feel sorry about it, we cannot help it. By default, the wait time is approximately three hours. Some days, the clinic closes at 10 a.m. due to the high volume of critical and emergency patients.

Everyone at the Beautiful Breath Clinic is very discerning. In other words, they excel at spotting and recognizing emergency patients. The receptionists in particular have a better eye than doctors who specialize in aesthetics.

As a private practice, the Beautiful Breath Clinic does not have an emergency room. Primary care institutions do not operate emergency rooms as part of their healthcare delivery system. The problem is that the Beautiful Breath Clinic receives many emergency patients.

I see patients in the office and exam room with not even 30 seconds to spare. I barely have time to go to the bathroom. The first person to greet a patient who comes to the Beautiful Breath Clinic is not a doctor, but a receptionist, which is not unique to our clinic. All primary care institutions and private practices have the same system. Imagine an emergency patient waiting for three hours without prompt care and treatment!

A patient's life could be lost. How did the receptionists at the Beautiful Breath Clinic develop the discernment to recognize emergency patients?

They are not doctors who graduated from medical school and trained in hospitals. Are new doctors naturally capable of diagnosing and treating emergency patients? Can they play the role of a doctor with only the knowledge they have learned from medical textbooks? Why does the medical school curriculum include hands-on training with patients? Healthcare cannot be learned from a book alone.
As patients are living beings, doctors experience a wide variety of
As patients are living beings, doctors experience a wide variety of situations with them. Medicine is one area that cannot be learned from books alone. The staff at the Beautiful Breath Clinic have been through a "rigorous training process" to develop discerning eyes. However, I know that no amount of rigorous training on its own could have made them as good as they are today. The staff members at the clinic care about the patients, just as the director does. Some staff members even care more about the patients than I do. These staff members work with the mindset that they need to save the patient even if the situation is critical.

A patient with very heavy breathing walked into the office before others in waiting. This patient had an acute exacerbation of bronchial asthma that could have resulted in severe sequelae or death if not treated within five minutes.
My instructions were followed and the patient passed the critical moment. At the reception desk in the waiting room, a patient had become furious and was yelling at a staff member. Having practiced respiratory medicine for most of my life, I have developed a dual personality. I have a rather hasty side to my personality, and I can get volatile. This makes sense, as many emergency patients can lose their lives in a matter of seconds.

How can I stay laid back when I do my job? My volatile personality comes out in situations like this. I walked right out into the noisy waiting room and asked what was going on. The angry patient was demanding to know why the other patient had gotten into the room first when he had arrived before that patient.

The staff member kindly explained that it was an emergency requiring immediate attention; however, the patient became even more upset. Treating and caring for emergency patients first is common sense and the right thing to do. In fact, it is even mandated by law.

Healthcare providers are liable if they do not treat emergency patients immediately. If there is only one doctor and two emergency patients arrive at the same time, the Medical Service Act prescribes that "the doctor must first give relief to the patient who is deemed to be in a more critical condition."

The patient's outburst and my response came almost simultaneously. The patient yelled at me. "I came all the way from Kazakhstan!" At about the same time, I shouted, "Go back to Kazakhstan then!" Later, I diagnosed and treated the patient as if we had never had such a heated argument. The patient apologized, and I also expressed my apologies. Another side of my personality is stillness.

When I come home to rest after a day of warfare in the clinic, I fall into a state of stillness and solitude where I feel like I am carrying the weight of the world on my shoulders alone.

I am worried about critical patients scheduled for the next day and cannot sleep at night, feeling an abysmal sense of loneliness when contemplating how I will get through another day.

The importance of discernment is not limited to doctors and hospital staff. Patients should also exercise discernment in choosing a doctor. Patients who lack medical experience often struggle to find a doctor who is right for them. Most local primary care doctors are likely quite good.

The safest bet for patients is to see a doctor at a hospital their local primary care doctor recommends. Doctors know doctors. They know who is the best and most qualified for the job. They recommend avoiding show doctors who advertise dietary supplements at all costs. True experts do not have time to go out and promote such products. They would rather write a paper, teach a class, or just relax if they have the time.

A great talent at the receptionist desk of the Beautiful Breath Clinic.
She is a combination of kindness, beauty, and wisdom.

Doctors' clinical experience matters. Expert doctors are likely to have excellent results on assessments by official, nationally recognized organizations. HIRA, which is responsible for objectively assessing the quality of medical care, has been providing assessment reports on the care and treatment of patients with respiratory diseases for more than 10 years.

What matters more than government assessments is the experience of patients. This is what we call "word of mouth." Doctors mean nothing without patients.

Registering patients and assessing symptoms in the main reception area of the Beautiful Breath Clinic.

04
The quintessential preaching to deaf ears

There is a famous proverb, "reading a scripture to cow's ears," which has the same meaning as "talking to a brick wall" or "preaching to deaf ears." The word "quintessential" describes the most essential part of a thing or phenomenon.

'The "quintessential preaching to deaf ears" is a state in which one cannot understand anything at all, no matter how many times it is explained to them. This book is not about learning proverbs. Why am I, a doctor rather than a teacher, mentioning this? I do so because I have seen this a lot in the clinic. What makes a doctor who diagnoses and treats patients talk about "preaching to deaf ears?" To illustrate this, here is my experience with a certain patient.

This 42-year-old female patient came to the Beautiful Breath Clinic with a cough that had been going on for more than two months. She lived in Jeju-do, an island, and traveled from there to the Beautiful Breath Clinic in Anam-dong, Seongbuk-gu, Seoul. Coughing for more than two months is very distressing. However, although coughing is a common symptom of many respiratory illnesses, it can also occur with a simple cold.

Specifically, coughs are divided into acute and chronic, depending on how long they last. Coughs lasting less than three weeks are classified as acute, and those lasting more than eight weeks are classified as chronic. The reason for the distinction between "acute" and "chronic" is that they often have different underlying conditions and therefore require different treatments.

Here is an important medical secret. Considering the definition of chronic cough is a cough that lasts for more than eight weeks, every patient with a chronic cough technically goes through a period of acute cough that lasts for three weeks.

Coughing, which is a symptom of many respiratory diseases, progresses from an acute cough to a chronic cough. Therefore, it is important not to make the mistake of ruling out the possibility of a respiratory disease associated with chronic cough because it has not been a full two months since the patient started coughing.

Many doctors make this error.

Many doctors make this error. I diagnosed the 42-year-old patient with non-asthmatic eosinophilic bronchitis (NAEB) and treated her accordingly. NAEB is a very unfamiliar diagnosis, even for doctors. The patient had probably never heard of such a diagnosis.

In the past, medical terminology and the names of diagnoses and treatments were often so confusing that patients and guardians who were not doctors often lacked an understanding of the disease. This is because modern medical terminology often originates from Latin, and the process of translating English into Korean often results in difficult medical terms. This patient did not understand the diagnosis either.

Even if patients have difficulties understanding a diagnosis, doctors should not replace it with which the patient is familiar. The name of this diagnosis clearly states that it is not asthma. Asthma can be excluded as a possibility since the condition is non-asthmatic. It includes bronchitis, thereby identifying it as bronchitis rather than not asthma. However, there is an additional term that can complicate this: "eosinophilic." Eosinophils are a type of white blood cell that plays a role in allergic reactions.

This diagnosis can now be accurately summarized as bronchitis caused by allergies and not asthma. I explained this to the 42-year-old patient at least three times, even writing and drawing on a sheet of paper. The patient asked several questions as she listened to my explanation, and I answered them at least three times and prescribed a treatment. There was nothing wrong so far.

The diagnosis may sound a little intimidating, but it is not a difficult for a pulmonologist to diagnose and treat. In fact, it is a very common condition, although the diagnosis itself is relatively new and neither doctors nor patients are familiar with it.

It is common enough to be one of the top four causes of chronic coughing. The patient from Jeju-do returned to the clinic two weeks later, and from the moment she walked in the door, she looked angry. She said she was there to claim damages for my misdiagnosis.
Unable to comprehend such nonsense, I asked. "Dear patient, may I beg your pardon? What do you mean by a claim for damages?"
The patient, who was diagnosed and treated for NAEB at the Beautiful Breath Clinic, went to the largest general hospital in Jeju-do when her cough did not improve. The doctor who treated her at the hospital allegedly gave diagnosed her with "hypersensitivity pneumonitis."

Hypersensitivity pneumonitis is an inflammatory disease of the lungs caused by an overreaction to allergens in fine organic dust. This is an entirely different condition from my diagnosis of NAEB.
Although allergic reactions are involved in both, hypersensitivity pneumonitis is an inflammation of the lungs whereas NAEB is an inflammation of the bronchi. Thus, the anatomical location of the disease is different. Although inflammation of the lungs and inflammation of the bronchi often occur together, they are technically two different conditions.

'However, interestingly, they are different diseases with the same treatment. The patient assumed that between "bronchitis" and "pneumonitis," one was a clear misdiagnosis. I could understand the patient's thought process. Nevertheless, being human, I recognized that I could be wrong.
Although the treatment for both conditions was the same, if my diagnosis was wrong the first time, I was willing to admit it and

apologize. I saw a chest CT scan from the hospital in Jeju-do. Hypersensitivity pneumonitis is a condition in which repeated exposure to organic dust (microscopic particles derived from animals and plants and contaminated by microorganisms such as fungi and bacteria). Subsequently, this can reach the peripheral regions of the lungs far from the bronchi, causing an overreaction (immune response) to allergens in the dust. This results in acute and chronic inflammation of the parenchyma of the lungs, including the alveoli and terminal bronchioles. There are characteristic findings of inflammation in the chest CT scan, an imaging test; however, this patient's chest CT showed no such evidence.

I explained to her that it was not hypersensitivity pneumonitis and there must have been a misunderstanding at the Jeju-do hospital. However, the patient had already made up her mind. No matter how many times I explained it to her, she continued to argue.

She asked for a refund for the tests she had at the Beautiful Breath Clinic. The more outrageous demands were for reimbursement for round-trip airfare from Jeju-do to Seoul and round-trip taxi fare from the airport to the clinic. Her demands did not stop there. She wanted me to also pay her for the babysitting costs while she was in and out of the clinic and compensate for her emotional distress.

In summary, her claims included a refund of the examination fee, reimbursement of transportation expenses, reimbursement of childcare expenses, and compensation for her emotional distress. I had at that point seen patients over 2 million times in 23 years, and this was the first time I had ever experienced such outrageous demands. I declined them all.

The diagnosis of NAEB was correct and was followed by appropriate treatment. The doctor in Jeju-do misdiagnosed her. The patient went on a rant, but backed down after my stern warning (interference with medical practice). I had a feeling she would not just go away that easily. The patient, who happened to work at a law firm in Jeju-do, was determined to annoy me in every way possible. She filed complaints with the health center and the National Human Rights Commission and a report to HIRA. Here complaints were all rejected. There was something the patient did not know.

As the director of the Beautiful Breath Clinic, I was an expert in dealing with such malicious complaints. Most patients have a good relationship with their doctors. However, any profession that deals with people encounters "obnoxious clients" from time to time. Doctors meet "obnoxious patients," as she was patient was one of them. Usually, I do not react to them since they are ill.

However, what doctors can and cannot tolerate is clear. I do not expect to be thanked for accurate diagnosis and treatment, but suing the clinic for compensation and reporting to multiple organizations is not about just harassing a single "doctor" who genuinely cares about his or her patients. Such behavior from ignorant people has led to a social phenomenon of avoiding essential healthcare. Eventually, the patient's complaint made its way to the Medical Dispute Mediation Committee.

The Korea Medical Dispute Mediation and Arbitration Agency (K-Medi) was founded in 2012. This patient, who claimed to work for a law firm and have legal knowledge, filed a complaint against the Beautiful Breath Clinic with K-Medi that suggested that supposed legal knowledge was quite limited. Complaints filed with the Medical Dispute Committee are automatically dropped if the doctor refuses to respond. To ensure a response from the doctor, the patient should have filed a complaint with the Korea Consumer Agency (KCA), not K-Medi.

Although I was not obligated to respond to the patient's complaint, as she did not know the difference between these legal mechanisms, I filled out the questionnaire in detail and submitted the necessary test data and evidence of treatment.

This was an extreme hassle for me, as I am very busy in the clinic every day and responsible for examining and treating critically ill patients. However, if I ignored it to avoid a hassle, the patient would mistake her false claims for the truth and would repeat the same misbehavior at other clinics in the future.

The Medical Dispute Mediation Committee does not make decisions based on one person's opinion. It is composed of at least six experts, including those from different disciplines of the medical community, civil society organizations, and lawyers. The expert doctor associated with the complaint is expected to complete and send in a very specific and appropriate questionnaire. This is not merely a formality.

These mediation decisions are also more detailed than court decisions, and the reasons for each mediation decision are very specific. The Mediation Committee provides their decisions based on specific medical explanations of the diagnosis treatment processes.

The Mediation Committee rejected all the complainant's claims, just as I expected. It felt great. The decision was also sent in writing to the complainant, and I could just imagine the look on the patient's face when she received the official letter listing the reasons for each of her demands being dismissed.

She could file a civil lawsuit against the decision of the Mediation Committee. Nevertheless, no lawyer in the world would take on a case like this, where the members of the Mediation Committee were unanimous in their medical opinions.

It was the verdict, and no amount of lawyering could overturn the medical facts. Medical facts are objective and scientific. They are truths that cannot be changed through persuasion.

'This experience was exactly like preaching to deaf ears. How frustrating and infuriating would it be to preach to deaf ears. However, I was neither frustrated nor infuriated.

I have had hundreds of experiences like this in my 30 years as a doctor. Patients could have suffered an injustice, and there may have been a "medical error" or "medical malpractice." However, both medical errors and malpractice refer to situations in which something bad happens to a patient or goes wrong with their health.

The severe chronic cough of the 42-year-old female patient from Jeju-do was cured in two weeks with my treatment. She was not harmed, and the exact cause of the cough that was bothering her was found and treated properly.

Why did the patient want to harass me so badly? As I am not a mind reader, I do not know her exact reasons.

I can only speculate that this is just how she is. The patient may have been upset by the term "pneumonitis" from the doctor in Jeju-do. However, I, the person who diagnosed her, was a pulmonologist specializing in treating patients with respiratory diseases, whereas the doctor in Jeju-do was a family medicine specialist. I am not talking about whether a treatment is good or bad. In medicine, experience matters, and when it comes to diagnosing and treating respiratory diseases, a "pulmonologist" is someone with more experience and medical knowledge than other types of doctors.

Why didn't she listen to the expert?

Perhaps she disbelieved the unfamiliar diagnosis of NAEB and was misled by the easy diagnosis of pneumonitis. A lesson can be learned from this patient's attitude. She was not even diagnosed with the common type of pneumonia with which most people are familiar. She was misdiagnosed with "hypersensitivity pneumonitis" to be exact.

Hypersensitivity pneumonitis is almost as unfamiliar a diagnosis as NAEB. Hypersensitivity pneumonitis has recently been renamed in Korean. NAEB could sound difficult, so I explained it in detail several times, like preaching to deaf ears. She misunderstood, misinterpreted, and misbehaved because she chose to keep wearing her deaf ears.

Doctors and patients do not have an equal level of medical expertise. The medical knowledge and experience of a pulmonologist who has practiced in the field of respiratory medicine for nearly a lifetime is not even comparable to that of a patient.

There is something called the 20,000-hour rule, which suggests that it takes at least 20,000 hours of practice to be an expert in a certain field. I have spent more than 200,000 hours as a specialist in examining, diagnosing, and treating patients in respiratory medicine. Just think about that—200,000 hours!

After spending more than 200,000 hours caring for respiratory patients, how could I have missed "hypersensitivity pneumonitis" if it was there? The patient's incomprehensible attitude was beyond puzzling to the point of being baffling to anyone with a modicum of common sense. Financial damage was incurred by the woman who made me experience the quintessential example of preaching to deaf ears. I hope she does not just regret the financial loss. The patient seemed to be living with a completely distorted outlook on life. I hope this served as lesson that pushed her to make a positive turn in her narrow-minded and paranoid worldview.

05
The paradox of prognosis

The word prognosis comes from the Greek words "pro" (before) and "gnosis" (to know) and refers to the course and outcome of a disease or patient. When a doctor examines a patient and predicts the course of a disease, it involves a very important medical judgment.

The difference between a patient being treated by a doctor who knows the natural course of a disease and a doctor who does not is as great as the differences between Heaven and Earth. Treating patients with a holistic view of their disease is closely related to improving their quality of life and reducing the frequency of possible complications.

The medical knowledge and experience that helps you understand that responses to treatment vary and disease progression can change drastically in speed and direction are even more important in areas of medicine where patients' lives are at stake.

Even the same disease can vary greatly depending on the patient's underlying medical conditions and age. The choice of which of many available treatments to use can determine whether a patient lives or dies. The prognosis of a diseases is also important for patients and guardians to know.

Healthcare is not a drama with a twist. While a drama or movie with a twist can be a masterpiece by giving the viewer or audience a sense of "unexpectedness," healthcare is all about predictable endings and processes.

Uncertainty and unpredictability can lead to extremely dangerous situations in healthcare. While there are different specialties of medical practice, all doctors expect predictable outcomes and rely on those predictions. The natural course and prognosis of disease are not the result of coincidence.

Modern medicine is built on a foundation of evidence, comprising a collection of data, cases, and experiments aggregated into statistics. For example, instead of treating pulmonary tuberculosis with a single drug, patients are given a combination of four drugs for the first two months, followed by a combination of three drugs for the next four months.

How is such a treatment regimen possible?

It has not been just studied in a hundred or a thousand patients. Instead, it is based on results that have been analyzed in tens of thousands, or even millions, of patients, based on different races, ages, and weights globally.

Pulmonary tuberculosis has existed as a disease since the beginning of human history, dating back at least to the 7th century BC. For a very long time, the cause of pulmonary tuberculosis remained unknown; therefore, it could not be cured. More people have died from pulmonary tuberculosis than from any other disease throughout history.

The same goes for lung cancer. It took a lot of research and hard work to uncover the causes of lung cancer and make breakthroughs in its treatment. Today, medical advances are still being made in the treatment of lung cancer.

A competent doctor will discuss the prognosis when treating a patient. A doctor who can provide an accurate prognosis is a complete expert on the disease and knows what can happen to the patient if a treatment is not provided or is unsuccessful.

Patients have the right to have their condition explained to them by their doctor, and doctors have a duty to provide those explanations.

An 80-year-old female patient had a persistent cough and sputum for 40 years—about half her life. She visited several hospitals and tried various folk remedies and medications prescribed by the hospital, but to no avail.

She eventually underwent a surgical resection of part of her left lung; however, the constant sputum continued. Eventually, she gave up trying. Three months ago, she started having a very large amount of yellow sputum, some with blood. She was short of breath and had tightness in her chest and a bad cough. The patient came to the Beautiful Breath Clinic after watching my lecture on bronchiectasis on the medical YouTube channel "@aftertherainkr."

> **The New England Journal of Medicin (NEJM)**
> is one of the world's leading medical journals.
>
> ## Seven Reasons to Treat Bronchiectasis
>
> SEONGLIM JIN, Director of the Beautiful Breath Clinic
> December 2, 2023 Saturday 8 p.m. - 10 p.m.

Clinical Review of Bronchiectasis in the NEJM.

When doctors see a patient, they first observe how the patient looks. This is known as visual observation. As soon as I saw her walk through the door, I had a gut feeling she had a serious respiratory condition. I did not need a stethoscope to listen to her breathing, which was crackling with sputum and making a wheezing sound.

Her breathing was labored to the extent that she had to use her assisted breathing muscles. Her complexion was pale, and she appeared extremely frail. It did not take any tests to recognize that she had very severe bronchiectasis. After the examination, one critical condition was added—pneumonia. It was pneumonia in an 80-year-old patient with severe bronchiectasis, and there was a high risk of progression to fatal pneumonia. I explained the patient's condition in detail to her guardian (husband) who had accompanied her.

I explained what treatment would be given, that treatment could put her at risk, and what could happen without it.

Usually, guardians are grateful to hear such an explanation. It is normal to ask the doctor to treat the patient well. However, this patient's guardian had a very unusual reaction and was suddenly angry with me. He yelled, "What kind of doctor are you to say that to a patient? Doctors should only say nice things to their patients! What risk are you talking about!"

At first, I was startled and did not quite understand what the guardian was talking about. However, it did not take long for me to realize what the guardian meant. He expressed offensive words and behavior again. Having seen patients more than two million times, I have met the oddest patients and guardians, as well as those who say the strangest things.

This was a special case. Her husband, the guardian, seemed to have trouble walking and was using a cane. It was no ordinary cane, but it was very thick and huge. He was furious and wielding the cane like a sword, posing a greater threat than he would have if he had been fumbling with a knife.

I never turn away when I encounter an unaware patient or guardian who does this to me or my clinic staff. I did not do anything wrong or need to apologize for any mistakes. Rather, as a doctor, I found the explanation very appropriate and professional.

The only thing I can do when facing an overexcited guardian is to get overexcited myself. Self-defense. However, as I responded without carrying any weapons, it was passive self-defense. I cannot simply respond in a whisper while my opponent wields a cane like a weapon and yells at me, can I? Would running away not make the situation even more ridiculous?

I am that type of person. I could have been assaulted, but I did not back down. I responded with a hard line. The doctor-patient relationship was already broken, and I could not treat the patient under these circumstances.

If left untreated, the patient could lose her life. I filled out a referral form to the department of pulmonology at the university hospital with the copies of the examination data and dismissed them.

'For the first time in my 30 years as a doctor, I wrote the following on a referral form:

"I have a patient with severe bronchiectasis, which on examination is accompanied by pneumonia requiring intravenous antibiotic therapy. As a severe conflict with the patient's guardian has compromised the patient-doctor relationship, I am referring the patient to your pulmonology department and attaching the imaging results."

I had not seen what was coming after explaining the prognosis. The guardian's words and behavior were very absurd. What had I done to deserve such absurdity? What about my words and actions? How could I tell the guardian the prognosis for the patient's disease to make it more palatable?

Would he have preferred to have her severe pneumonia described as a mild cold and be told not to worry as she would be all better with treatment? If I had comforted them with such an elaborate explanation, there would have been an unparalleled uproar if the patient's pneumonia had gotten worse, blaming me for not making an accurate prediction.

I believe no words I could say would make this type of guardian happy. This was a person whose life was full of complaints and gripes, no matter where he was or what he was going through. I did not have to tolerate his complaints or feel intimidated by his threats. This type of guardian could easily do the same thing at any hospital. It must have been the first time he was stopped by a strong protest and warning and could have been a shock to him.

Shouting and waving a cane like that old man is not the way to deal with the problems in our world. Age is nothing but a number. Some remain childish and foolish the older they get, whereas others grow more mature and wiser with age. The truth is that you are responsible for your words and actions.

"If you can't stand the heat, get out of the kitchen." "You can lead a horse to the water, but you can't make him drink." I cannot hold onto a patient who refuses to be treated. Technically, the patient did not refuse to get treatment.

The old man engaged in a very serious action that legally constituted "special intimidation." Intimidation is the act of threatening someone with the intent to make them do something. In South Korean criminal law, intimidation is defined as a threat to harm another person's life, body, honor, or property in order to cause fear.

The more serious offense of special intimidation refers to intimidating a group or multiple groups by showing force or carrying a dangerous object and is punishable by imprisonment for up to seven years or a fine of up to KRW 10 million.

Moreover, the situation at university hospitals would make it difficult to find a place to treat severe pneumonia. I was concerned about the patient, and if she came back, I would have liked to reconcile with her guardian to provide prompt treatment for her pneumonia and bronchiectasis. They say that you lose patience as you get older. Patients are always the underdog, are they not?

I hope the old female patient recovers well.

A paradox is an argument that appears to make sense on the surface but is actually contradictory. The guardian may have thought he was right, but in the end, he made a very bad choice.

06
The truth and lies of HIRA healthcare quality assessment

South Korea's healthcare system is a mandatory designation system. This system mandates that all hospitals and clinics in South Korea accept patients with medical insurance.

If a doctor wants to stop seeing insured patients and only see uninsured patients, they cannot do so. The mandatory designation system has been in place for decades following the Constitutional Court's ruling that although it conflicted with the constitutional spirit of freedom of occupational choice, it was permissible to restrict the occupational choice of certain professions (doctors) in the interest of public health.

A healthcare system with a mandatory designation system has two major organizations. One is the National Health Insurance Service and the other is HIRA. HIRA's role is to review whether the medical testing methods doctors use to diagnose patients are adequate and whether the injections or drugs they use for treatment are appropriate.

Many of those who work at HIRA are not medically trained and have never seen a patient in a medical setting. In layman's terms, the actions of an expert doctor are reviewed by non-expert HIRA employees based on the standards of HIRA.

The judgment of HIRA is primarily manifested in the act of "cutting." Although it is no longer described as a cut but as an "adjustment of healthcare fees," it means the same thing. HIRA refuses to pay hospitals for services if doctors have not followed th4e guidelines set forth by HIRA as a result of a later quality assessment of the blood tests, imaging tests, injections, or medications used to diagnose and treat a patient with pneumonia.

This is quite common. Doctors use their medical judgment to do whatever is best for their patients, but they are not paid for their services. It would be like selling ten baskets of fruit at the market and then having an official from the Ministry of Agriculture and Fisheries come out and demand the cost of the fruit be refunded to the Ministry of Agriculture and Fisheries, accusing you of selling good fruit at a high price to consumers.

The key here is "good fruit" and "high price." Based on such logic, you are only allowed to sell "bad fruit" at a low cost to consumers. Does this reasoning make sense?

The same thing is happening in healthcare. A guiding principle of HIRA to provide "low-cost treatment" with "low-cost medicine." If doctors ignore this principle and treat with "good medicine" at "high cost," HIRA will not pay them.

HIRA must have determined that cuts alone are insufficient to reduce healthcare costs. Recently, HIRA introduced the concept of healthcare appropriateness assessment, evaluating the use of certain medications for certain conditions and recognizing outstanding healthcare institutions.

Appropriateness assessments have contributed greatly to the standardization of healthcare quality and safe treatment of patients. I think the program works very well, and it has been statistically proven. South Korea used to have a very high antibiotic prescription rate. Starting with an assessment of antibiotic prescribing rates in 2001, the program has expanded to include acute and chronic illnesses and cancer. In June 2023, Article 47(4) of the National Health Insurance Act was newly enacted to clarify the legal basis for the appropriateness assessment and ensure the assessment system can operate efficiently.

The new appropriateness assessment will incorporate treatment success rates (within one year of diagnosis) as an indicator for monitoring and measuring the performance of care, as opposed to the standardized diagnosis driven by the highest tuberculosis incidence rates among countries in the Organization for Economic Cooperation and Development (OECD).

As a pulmonologist, I believe that the appropriateness assessment of the standard treatment for tuberculosis has been a very successful and beneficial program. In a country where the incidence of tuberculosis has been at the top of the OECD for more than 40 years and where many people continue to struggle with tuberculosis, I believe that the appropriateness assessment has contributed to the correct diagnosis and treatment of tuberculosis by setting the standard. Seeing inhaled inhaler therapy as the first-line and most important treatment for bronchial asthma and COPD, as well as regular pulmonary function tests as a monitoring indicator in the evaluation, is gratifying.

Efforts by the Korean Academy of Tuberculosis and Respiratory Diseases and HIRA's appropriateness assessment of asthma care are yielding good results in increasing prescribing rates for inhaled inhaler therapy. However, the antibiotic prescribing appropriateness assessment for lower respiratory tract conditions to be implemented this year is of great concern. Lower respiratory tract disease refers to conditions in the lower bronchi and alveoli. Infections of the lower bronchi are often treated with antibiotics, and the most common lower respiratory tract infections include pneumonia, bronchiectasis, and chronic mucopurulent bronchitis.

These illnesses are often accompanied by chronic respiratory disease, and patients tend to be in critical condition. Treatment for these patients cannot rely on a short course of cheap antibiotics. In fact, this would only increase the risk of antibiotic resistance.

Treatment of patients with lower respiratory tract infections should consist of the generous use of "expensive antibiotics." I do not understand the monitoring metrics in the appropriateness assessment for lower respiratory tract antibiotics. I would like to ask what specialist they consulted to make this decision. I wonder if the monitoring metrics were determined after consultation and discussion with a pulmonologist who has sufficient clinical experience with lower respiratory tract patients in clinical settings.

The Beautiful Breath Clinic has never failed to receive the highest possible rating of level 1 in the appropriateness assessments for the diagnosis and treatment of asthma and COPD. It is also rated level 1 for antibiotic prescription for upper respiratory disease and for the treatment of hypertension.

However, it was rated level 5—the lowest level of appropriateness—or the prescription of lower respiratory tract antibiotics. Why was it rated 5 for lower respiratory tract infections? My skills are intact. Patients with lower respiratory tract infections present in very critical condition.

The guidelines for the use of antibiotics in the lower respiratory tract are based on mild lower respiratory tract infections sometimes see at local doctor's offices. The severity of the condition of the patients on which the basic judgment is based is completely different from the condition of patients at my clinic.

A short course of mild antibiotics is appropriate for patients with a mild lower respiratory tract infection. No skilled pulmonologist would prescribe a third-generation cephalosporin antibiotic or a fourth-generation quinolone antibiotic to a patient with a mild lower respiratory tract infection, much less a combination (prescribing two antibiotics together) of a cephalosporin antibiotic and a macrolide antibiotic or of a cephalosporin antibiotic and a quinolone antibiotic.

However, what happens when a patient with a severe lower respiratory tract infection is prescribed a short course of mild antibiotics? The patient could lose their life.

Suppose the patient died when the doctor followed the HIRA guidelines for treatment. Do you think a court would hold HIRA, that developed the guidelines, accountable and not the doctor?

What would we do with patients whose lives are lost and their families beyond the discussion of legal accountability? Would HIRA take responsibility?

Healthcare is not something that is determined like grabbing a drink from an off-the-shelf vending machine.

Patients' clinical manifestations are highly variable and may harbor multiple conditions simultaneously, complicating treatment. It is wrong and dangerous to develop an appropriateness assessment as a multiple-choice questionnaire based on some armchair theory asking you to pick a number from 1 to 5.

Patients are organic, and you never know when an unexpected event will arise. Critically ill patients can be saved with proactive treatment before their condition worsens.

The HIRA guidelines of using first-line antibiotics first, followed by second-line antibiotics if they do not work, followed by third- and fourth-line antibiotics if they still do not work, is the very thing causing the antibiotic resistance. Moreover, critically ill patients would be killed in the process. By the time you get to the second- and third-line antibiotics, the patient may have already died. Thus, I completely ignore the HIRA guidelines on antibiotics when seeing critically ill patients.

I ignore them to save the patients. Following them would cost patients their lives.

HIRA has sent me a letter stating that if I continue to show a lack of improvement to the antibiotic appropriateness in my treatment of lower respiratory tract infections, they will investigate my clinic for improvement after consulting with experts.

I have no idea who they are going to bring in to review when I happen to be the best expert.

If I have a patient in front of me with a lower respiratory tract infection who is collapsing and could die of pneumonia, would I be able to treat them according to the HIRA appropriateness guidelines for lower respiratory tract infections? Would the HIRA employees or their families want to receive treatment according to HIRA guidelines if they had a lower respiratory tract infection?

In a world of limited insurance resources, no doctor would object to treating patients with cheap medicines if they work well. However, if the outcome is affected and the patient's life is at stake, the story is different.

Doctors are not puppets of HIRA. Doctors diagnose and treat patients based on their own opinions and judgment. Becoming a pulmonologist takes 16 years of hard work.

This is not something in which non-experts should interfere. Doctors have the inherent authority to know what is best for their patients and decide which medications to use when treating them. The HIRA guidelines are never the standard by which patients should be treated. The choice of antibiotic, its dose, combination, and duration of use should be made by doctors, period.

Chapter 4

Mind your Ps and Qs

No good deed goes unpunished

Uninvited Guests

Drug Utilization Review(DUR)

Reality and illusion of symptoms

01
Mind your Ps and Qs

The phrase "mind your Ps and Qs" means that you should be careful about what you say or do.

It implies that the same thing can be said differently depending on who is saying it. It also suggests that many factors, such as the speaker's position, the listener's situation, emotions, and mindset, can greatly influence the content of what is spoken and how words are expressed. This means that the same thing can be conveyed very differently depending on how people deliver it. Words are not just a means of conveying information but a tool reflecting the mindset, emotions, and values of the speaker and conveying various meanings and emotions to the listener.

A 67-year-old female patient presented with a very severe cough, shortness of breath, and purulent sputum. Coughing, shortness of breath, and sputum are symptoms of many different respiratory conditions.

Given her history of over 10 years with these symptoms, this was not an acute condition. It must have been a chronic respiratory disease. Chronic respiratory diseases should be treated by first identifying the cause. Imaging studies and bronchoscopy were performed. Bronchoscopy revealed very severe purulent sputum in the bilateral lower lobe bronchi, and the bronchial mucosa was edematous and dilated with a long history of chronic inflammation. Sputum was stuck in the bronchial tubes like a foreign body, blocking the breathing passages, making it difficult to breathe, and causing a grunting sound that gets louder when lying down at night.

Her bronchiectasis was old, poorly treated, and very severe. I cleared out all the sputum inside the bronchi. The collection and removal of sputum is clinically important, as sputum is used for various microbiological tests.

Microbiologic testing is important because patients with bronchiectasis are often infected with bacteria, tuberculosis bacilli, fungi, and non-tuberculous mycobacteria. The causative bacteria are important to pinpoint for antibiotic susceptibility testing to determine if the bacteria will respond well to antibiotics. Knowing which bacteria respond well to which antibiotics is essential for accurate treatment. Furthermore, patients with bronchiectasis are likely to have colonized bacteria owing to prolonged exposure, and the bacteria are often virulent and antibiotic-resistant. Routine bacterial cultures and antibiotic susceptibility tests take a week to produce results. I had the patient back a week after the test.

"Dear patient, we have a culture of a very virulent bacteria called pseudomonas, but I am happy to report that they respond well to antibiotics."

"Doctor, I heard that I had no bacteria."

What was she talking about? I asked in response, "No bacteria?"

The patient made it very clear. She said that a staff member at the clinic explained there were no findings. I knew no staff member at the clinic would make such a mistake. I explained again and insisted that no employee at the clinic would say that there were no findings when there were. The patient said she was told this over the phone.

I was puzzled. When I asked her if she knew the name of the employee who explained it, she said she did not. However, it did not take long to clear up the confusion.

It turned out that the patient had forgotten that her results would come back in a week and called the clinic three days after the tests to inquire about the results. No bacterial culture is available three days after the test. The staff member who took the call explained that there were no results, meaning that the test results were not ready, and it would take four more days to get them. The patient misunderstood the staff member's words there being no bacterial findings in the test results. It was a typical "Ps and Qs" situation. It really showed the importance of clearly distinguishing Ps from Qs.

This type of experience is very common in the clinic. Doctors should be mindful of their language. They must make clear statements using the proper emphasis. Patients are focused on their own disease and do not know as much about medical terms or conditions as doctors do.

The staff at the clinic always makes sure to provide accurate explanations.

Therefore, when doctors explain their disease, treatments, possible adverse events, and expected outcomes, patients often hear only what they want to hear and misinterpret things. Informed consent is obtained for major tests or procedures and the form provides details in writing and leaves no room for misunderstanding, but spoken words are something else entirely.

I cannot record every conversation I have with patients in my practice either. These days, it is not uncommon for patients to make a recording or capture a video of their doctor's explanation.

Some patients feel guilty about recording, so they do it secretly. They may think that they are being stealthy, but you can tell when they are recording. In those situations, I tell the patient not to be uncomfortable and to feel free to record the conversation or make a video. Doctors do not need to be offended by such behavior. In fact, in some situations, it may be safer for doctors to videotape or record a procedure.

The practice of medicine starts with mutual trust between the doctor and patient; however, in the cut-throat modern world, things can easily turn into legal disputes. Recent court decisions are different from past cases, when patients had to find and prove a doctor's wrongdoing to win a case. Recently, however, doctors have needed to prove that they did nothing wrong to win.

Therefore, doctors should document in the medical records any conversations they have with patients, their symptoms, whether any tests are recommended, and if patients have refused any recommended tests.

The same is true for follow-ups. For example, if a low-dose chest CT scan reveals a small nodule (less than 3 cm) in the lungs, a follow-up scan should be done after a few months (from as short as 3-6 months to as long as 12 months).

If doctors only verbally explain this to the patient and do not document it in the medical records, they could be held liable if something goes wrong later. To be fair, simply keeping a note in the medical records is nothing more than a defense mechanism for doctors.

A good hospital should have a system that schedules patient visits six months in advance and sends a text to the patient's mobile when the date arrives. The primary responsibility for remembering to come in for the six-month checkup lies with the patient. However, in the busyness of modern life, patients may forget the date, and even if they do remember it, they may not realize the importance of the test and skip it. This is why hospitals' scheduling and patient notification systems are so important.

The medical field is not the only place we need to mind our "Ps" and "Qs." There is also a fundamental lesson in human relations. We all make "self-serving" decisions as the human instinct is to be selfish. However, being selfish is not necessarily a bad thing, and could even be a good thing. If you do not look out for yourself, who is going to do it? Selfishness is bad when it deprives others of benefits or if you hurt others to benefit yourself. However, taking care of yourself without harming others is important.

People with high self-esteem value themselves. Self-esteem is a very important when moving through life. People with high self-esteem do not deliberately misinterpret the words of others to their advantage. They try to understand the relationship and situation accurately to capture the essence of what others are trying to convey.

A classic "Ps" and "Qs" situation could make a fun anecdote. Sometimes, these situations are remembered as fun stories that bring big laughs. Such an experience can form some of the fondest memories in the hustle and bustle of life.

Where there is light, there are shadows; where there is day, there is night; and where there is meeting, there is parting.

Is that not what life is all about? A "Ps and Qs" situation can end up as a fun little episode as long as no one makes a big deal out of it. Anger or frustration over such misunderstandings is unnecessary.

However, in the context of making a critical decision or choice, you may not take it lightly. In the crossroads of the weights and choices, it may pay to mind your "Ps" and "Qs."

02
No good deed goes unpunished

A 78-year-old man came to the clinic with hemoptysis (blood in sputum). Hemoptysis is among the most concerning symptoms of respiratory diseases. Patients presenting with hemoptysis may have any of several conditions that range from mild to severe. This symptom is most often associated with respiratory diseases but can also occur in non-respiratory conditions. Nosebleeds are not called hemoptysis, and it is also differentiated from hematemesis, which is vomiting blood from the gastrointestinal tract.

The definition of medically significant massive hemoptysis varies somewhat across medical schools, but is generally defined as hemoptysis of 100-600 cc or more per day. Massive hemoptysis is a medical emergency, accounting for 1.5-5% of all hemoptysis cases. In particular, the rate of hemoptysis is more important than the total amount, as hemoptysis at a rate of 100 cc/hour is associated with a risk of asphyxiation or shock, requiring urgent medical attention.

Common causes of hemoptysis include bronchiectasis, malignant tumors, chronic bronchitis, tuberculosis, and pulmonary arteriovenous malformations originating in the pulmonary arteries. Additionally, a special form of hemoptysis, called diffuse alveolar hemorrhage, occurs various respiratory diseases.

In addition to respiratory diseases, there is also heart disease, valve disease, and a rare condition called pulmonary endometriosis, which only occurs during a woman's period.

Patients who smoke, are older than 70 years of age, and have hemoptysis are at increased risk of developing lung cancer. These patients needed a thorough examination of the lungs and bronchi. Bronchoscopy is required in conjunction with imaging tests. The patient had a tumor in his lungs and was diagnosed with squamous cell carcinoma after bronchoscopic biopsy.

Squamous cell carcinoma refers to a variety of cancers that start in the squamous cells of the human body and can appear as esophageal, skin, and vaginal cancer, besides being a type of lung cancer. For squamous cell lung cancer, surgery is the mainstay of treatment when the cancer is stage IIIa or before; however, chemotherapy or radiation is used when the cancer has progressed to stage IIIb or IV. This patient had highly advanced stage IV lung cancer.

He had been to several other hospitals, but because he did not show any symptoms of hemoptysis, he was not given a thorough examination, missing the time for an early diagnosis of lung cancer. It was an unfortunate situation, but my clinic quickly and accurately confirmed the type and stage of his lung cancer.

I informed the patient and his guardian of the lung cancer diagnosis and recommended chemotherapy or radiation, as the tumor was inoperable. It was then that the guardian made a strange request. Really, it was more of a demand than a request. The guardian asked me to make an appointment at Seoul National University Hospital as soon as possible. At first, I completely understood the guardian's feelings. Who would be able to remain calm when their beloved father has been diagnosed with stage IV lung cancer?

I would have felt the same way if I were in the guardian's position. In fact, my own father was a lung cancer patient, and I was the one who diagnosed and confirmed his condition. My father had small cell carcinoma. He did not receive chemotherapy at Seoul National University Hospital. Small cell carcinoma is a very fast-growing lung cancer that can kill you before you can get chemotherapy at a major university hospital considering the long wait times.

Squamous cell carcinoma has a different prognosis than small cell carcinoma. I could empathize with the guardian because I was also a family member of a lung cancer patient. No good deed goes unpunished, and good deeds may not always pay off. There are people out there who make unreasonable requests or demands without shame.

This patient's guardian made increasingly unreasonable demands, which came across more like a threat. The guardian asked me to make an appointment at Seoul National University Hospital as soon as possible no matter what. I was the doctor who diagnosed the patient's lung cancer. Within five days of his arrival at our hospital, the histologic type and stage of his lung cancer was confirmed.
Even at a university hospital, lung cancer can take at least two to three weeks to diagnose, and more than two months during this time of healthcare crisis. Honestly speaking, the guardian and patient were lucky to have me.
Which private hospitals in South Korea can diagnose lung cancer? It is only possible at the Beautiful Breath Clinic.
In this situation, the patient's guardian kept urging me to make an appointment at Seoul National University Hospital as soon as possible. No amount of fussing and fuming could make it work. It took more than two months to get an appointment at Seoul National University Hospital, and it was beyond my control.
I had to convince the guardian that it would be better for the patient's survival and lessen his suffering to receive treatment at another university hospital sooner rather than wait two months for treatment at Seoul National University Hospital. The patient's guardian, who was stubborn, eventually gave up on Seoul National University Hospital.

I assumed the problem was solved; however, this time the guardian demanded a referral to Asan Medical Center. Did I look like a genie in a lamp? I was no Mary Poppins who could snap my fingers to make things work. It was not as easy as that.
The guardian may have thought that since a primary healthcare provider like my clinic correctly diagnosed their father's lung cancer, it would not be difficult for me to make an appointment at a university hospital. However, making an appointment at a university hospital has nothing to do with a doctor's skills.
Any university hospital has its own reservation system, and currently,

owing to the special circumstances surrounding the resignation of residents, making an appointment at a university hospital at will was impossible. After another lengthy argument, I was able to convince the guardian of this. To put it more precisely, I told them to face reality.

I had many friends when I was younger; however, as I grew older, my social circle shrank. My personality may not have been sufficiently attractive to keep them around. However, I have also had friends who have made unreasonable demands of me.

I had a very close friend. I had known him for 50 years, so we had been friends for quite a long time. However, I lost him, too. I cannot reveal the exact reason here, but I can say that my good deeds did not pay off. This friend did not just ask for a small favor, followed by a big one. He asked for a big favor and kept asking for even bigger favors. A friendship may be something that can be rebuilt over time, but my friendship with him became irreparable because he shamelessly continued to make unreasonable demands.

A sense of shame can be an important virtue in human relationships. One should be able to reflect on oneself and feel ashamed of any faults. Those who have shame have very different attitudes than those of people who are shameless. With too many shameless people roaming the world, a sense of shame is urgently needed.

There are also many shameless doctors out there. Patients should be wary of shameless doctors because their lives are at stake. Nothing is more precious than life.

Doctors should value their patients' lives more than their religious beliefs. Such a sense of professional ethics stems from an awareness of the nature of the profession of doctor.

03
Uninvited Guests

"Life is a journey full of uninvited guests."
This is not a quote from any philosopher but a view of life I have developed over 30 years of seeing patients. I realize how quickly time passes now that I have established a subjective view of life.

Doctors often receive unwanted guests. In particular, pulmonologists specializing in the diagnosis and treatment of human breathing encounter unpredictable patients. However, doctors in private dermatology or plastic surgery clinics specializing in aesthetics see invited patients. The nature of aesthetic procedures means that most patients undergo a consultation beforehand. Few unexpected events occur in aesthetic practice or treatment. Predictability with no surprises is bliss.

Healthcare is not a drama. Just as airplane pilots dread turbulence, doctors feel overwhelmed and frustrated when a patient's condition suddenly changes or when they encounter unexpected patients.

Some types of industries may welcome uninvited guests. If tickets to a sporting event or concert are not sold out, the hosting organization would be happy to welcome unscheduled audiences. A restaurant owner with unreserved empty tables would gladly welcome uninvited guests.

University hospitals—tertiary healthcare institutions—operate emergency rooms to treat unexpected patients quickly and accurately. Emergency medicine doctors in emergency departments have specialized medical knowledge and skills for dealing with unexpected visitors. Readers may think that emergency medicine doctors perform all medical procedures in an emergency room, which could be true or false. Emergency medicine doctors are the first to examine patients arriving at the emergency room and will diagnose and treat patients needing care. However, emergency medicine doctors do not treat all types of severe emergencies.

Patients with severe hip joint fractures should be referred to orthopedic surgeons for treatment, while those with severe exacerbations of pulmonary fibrosis should be referred to pulmonologists. Thus, competent emergency medicine doctors quickly diagnose emergency patients' conditions and refer them to the appropriate specialists. In the emergency room, emergency medicine doctors are like air traffic controllers who ensure airplanes fly safely while also being the pilots flying the airplanes.

Life is full of invited or uninvited guests. Invited guests can be interpreted as things that make people happy. Almost all people crave happiness and pleasure; only a small percentage enjoy pain. Nevertheless, happiness and pleasure are not spontaneous phenomena but can be achieved through patience and hard work. Even if you can find pleasure after hard work and suffering, it does not last forever.

Humans are forgetful beings, and the moment they become forgetful, they meet uninvited guests. Pleasure-seekers pursue greater stimulation, which can lead to intense pleasure as well as pain because of the human ability to adapt to any intense stimulus. In life, uninvited guests are inevitable. One can suddenly become sick or face an unexpected accident or even death. The reality of life is that everyone will die at some point along the way. Although physical pain is an uninvited guest that arrives out of nowhere, other uninvited guests can strike at the mind and heart.

A 24-year-old young woman presented with a shortness of breath that had persisted for six months. She was short of breath all day and made wheezing sounds. Wheezing is typically heard when listening to breath sounds with a stethoscope. However, occasionally, as with this patient, it can be heard without a stethoscope. If wheezing is audible without a stethoscope, it can also be heard with the patient's ears. With shortness of breath and wheezing, bronchial asthma is often the first probable diagnosis. This patient had been diagnosed with bronchial asthma at five different hospitals over six months and had taken oral medications, inhaler treatments, and injections.

If a disease is diagnosed correctly and the appropriate treatment is provided, the symptoms of the disease almost always improve, except in extremely unusual cases. This should be especially true with bronchial asthma, considering its reversible nature. However, this patient's symptoms had shown no improvement. A complete lack of response implied the diagnosis of bronchial asthma was incorrect. For a 24-year-old woman, it was a considerably painful uninvited guest.

I have said that doctors do not like uninvited guests, and the moment I saw this patient, I found this particular uninvited guest considerably familiar. Her symptoms indicated a condition I had seen countless times over the past 30 years. Why did the doctors at the other hospitals not diagnose this condition, which they might have seen many times on internal medicine exams in medical school? If the same question had been asked on an exam, many medical students would have given the correct answer. The misdiagnosis by the practicing doctors, who were more experienced than medical students, was because of a generalization of everyday experience instead of a lack of medical knowledge.

This patient had bronchial tuberculosis, not bronchial asthma. Pulmonary tuberculosis is characterized by the presence of tuberculous lesions on a chest radiograph, which allows for quick diagnosis. Pulmonary tuberculosis is not diagnosed by chest radiography. Confirming the presence of Mycobacterium tuberculosis by sputum examination is essential. Recently, there has been an increase in nontuberculous mycobacterial infections resembling tuberculosis, which must also be differentiated.

Bronchial asthma appears normal on a chest radiograph. Surprisingly, even with bronchial tuberculosis, the chest radiograph comes out normal. Even with a diagnosis of tuberculosis, the imaging tests appear normal.

Thus, how could I have suspected and diagnosed bronchial tuberculosis in this patient?

First, wheezing is not audible 24 hours a day in bronchial asthma. Bronchial asthma is characterized by narrowing and loosening of the bronchial tubes. The narrowing of the bronchi causes wheezing. Therefore, wheezing throughout the day is a symptom that should be a red flag for something other than bronchial asthma. Second, if it is bronchial asthma, the patient's symptoms should improve upon taking or inhaling asthma medication, as the response to asthma treatment is considerably good, especially in those as young as 24 years old. Third, asthma rarely produces excessive sputum.

The three symptoms above already suggested that this was not bronchial asthma. Given the similarity in symptoms to bronchial asthma and the patient's young age, bronchial tuberculosis should be suspected immediately, followed by bronchoscopy. The patient underwent bronchoscopy and was diagnosed with bronchial tuberculosis, which led to the initiation of treatment. Nevertheless, would the patient stop encountering uninvited guests once treatment for bronchial tuberculosis had started?

As a pulmonologist, I am aware of the after-effects of bronchial tuberculosis. I felt heavy-hearted. Bronchial tuberculosis is not as easy to diagnose quickly as pulmonary tuberculosis and is an individual problem. However, it is also a major health and sociological concern and more contagious than pulmonary tuberculosis. Younger people are more active and likely to move around and come into contact with others. Korea continues to rank first among OECD countries in the incidence of and number of deaths from tuberculosis.

The most dreaded unwelcome guest for these patients is bronchial stenosis, a permanent narrowing of the bronchi. Bronchial stenosis is a considerably scary, uninvited guest that can significantly reduce one's quality of life. The bronchial tubes are narrowed permanently and irreversibly, leaving patients with breathing difficulties for the rest of their lives. The only treatment for bronchial stenosis is to place a bronchial stent to widen the narrowed bronchus and prevent it from shrinking further. Nonetheless, bronchial stenting is not a permanent cure but a temporary solution associated with various adverse events.

I cross my fingers and pray that this young patient does not have the uninvited guest of "bronchial stenosis" in her life.

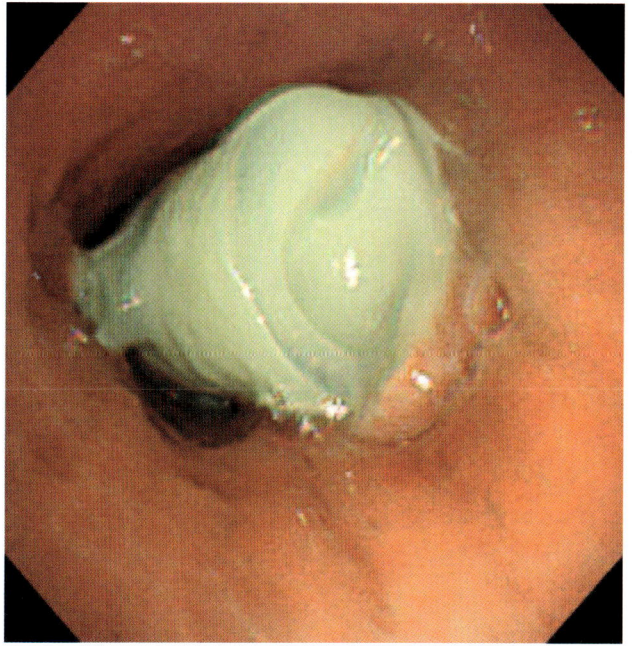

Photograph of a patient who developed bronchial stenosis as a sequela of bronchial tuberculosis and underwent bronchial stenting.

04
Drug Utilization Review(DUR)

A 47-year-old male patient had been suffering from insomnia and panic following a recent business failure. He wanted a prescription for sleeping pills and tranquilizers. Sleeping pills currently cannot be prescribed for more than 28 days. I gave the patient a 21-day prescription. Recently, nearly all hospitals and clinics have adopted an electronic medical record (EMR) program. EMR allows for quick and accurate documentation with various practice support programs that are more convenient than traditional medical records. It also connects online with the Health Insurance Review and Assessment Service (HIRA) to receive the drug utility review (DUR) service.

The DUR service is designed to provide real-time information related to drug safety, such as contraindications, when prescribing or dispensing drugs to prevent inappropriate drug use. If a doctor gives a prescription, it will be issued without problems. However, if the patient has already been prescribed sleeping pills at another hospital, a "DUR" pop-up will appear in the EMR. It provides the name of the hospital where the patient has already been prescribed, the date and time of the prescription, and how many pills they were prescribed. Such a system shows why South Korea is an Internet powerhouse. The DUR system is not triggered because sleeping pills are controlled substances.

Even better, it tells you which medications patients should not take together. For example, it will notify the doctor if a patient takes a cholesterol medication prescribed by a different provider. Although patients are obligated to tell their doctors what medications they are taking, it can be nearly impossible for patients to keep track of all their medications.

Patients may say they are allergic to a particular medication. Nevertheless, I have not seen patients who memorize all the medication prescriptions they take or keep a photo of them on their phone to share them with their doctor when they visit another hospital for a different condition. Previously, there have been issues with people taking medications that should not be taken together. The DUR system issues a warning notification when prescribing medications that should not be combined.

Antibiotics should be prescribed when a patient taking an anticholesterol medication has acute pneumonia, severe bronchitis, or bacterial inflammation of the sinuses. However, there are many different types of antibiotics, including macrolides, a popular class of antibiotics. Antibiotics in the macrolide class should not be combined with medications that lower cholesterol levels. Therefore, owing to the DUR system alert, doctors can switch the antibiotic they are about to prescribe to one that is cephalosporin-based, which could prevent adverse events from medications.

What an advanced system for a country of medical excellence! The DUR system has other advantages as well. Prior to its introduction, some patients would travel from one hospital to another to obtain medications. Theoretically, they could go to more than a hundred hospitals and take tens of thousands of drugs not classified as controlled or narcotic substances, such as blood pressure pills, diabetes pills, fever reducers, or antibiotics.

In the past, a few thoughtless patients and caregivers took advantage of this loophole to purchase hundreds of thousands of blood pressure pills cheaply with their health insurance and sell them online or offline for more money. The phenomenon of "hospital shopping" by patients has been around for a considerable period and continues today. However, no patient can currently be prescribed more blood pressure or diabetes medication than they need because the DUR system knows how many days of blood pressure medication a patient has been prescribed.

If a patient receives a six-month supply of blood pressure medication from "Kim's Clinic" and goes to "Park's Clinic" a month later to ask for another six-month supply of blood pressure medication, the doctor at Park's Clinic would not automatically know that the patient has already received a six-month supply of blood pressure medication from Kim's Clinic.

When the doctor believes the patient and enters a six-month supply of blood pressure medication into the electronic record, a DUR pop-up appears with a warning message. It will alert the doctor that the patient received a six-month supply of blood pressure medication from Kim's Clinic approximately a month earlier. This will prevent the doctor at Park's Clinic from prescribing blood pressure medication; nonetheless, there may be exceptions. For example, a patient who was given a six-month prescription for blood pressure medication by Kim's Clinic may be going on an urgent nine-month business trip overseas. In this case, the patient has taken one month of a six-month supply of blood pressure medication and, therefore, has a five-month supply of blood pressure medication remaining. In such a special case, the doctor at Park's Clinic would be allowed to prescribe an additional four-month supply of blood pressure medication. Nevertheless, the liability falls on the doctors if they prescribe unconditionally. The doctor may later be contacted to provide compensation for the entire cost of the blood pressure medication, as it has been prescribed in duplicate.

Currently, essential healthcare in South Korea is covered by the compulsory insurance designation system, including medical expenses through the National Health Insurance Service. Doctors must pay for the medications they have overprescribed unknowingly or knowingly. This system is not ideal. The pharmacy accepts the money for the medication, and the patient takes the medicine to control their illness. The doctors prescribe medications based on their diagnoses; however, the pharmacy, not the doctors, charges the patients for the prescribed medications.

However, doctors are held 100% financially responsible for

overprescribing or prescribing expensive antibiotics. Can you understand this? Can doctors practice medicine without compromising their convictions in such a system? Doctors want to treat patients quickly. Although expensive drugs are not always better, clear differences often exist, especially regarding antibiotics, which come in many classes. Expensive antibiotics should not be used for mild cases primarily because of the critical problem of antibiotic resistance rather than economic concerns. Nevertheless, using cheap antibiotics in severely ill patients can put them at risk, which, economically speaking, is an even bigger loss.

If an expensive antibiotic is administered immediately to a critically ill patient and the patient's condition improves in a week, the cost would be approximately KRW 300,000. A week of inexpensive antibiotics for a severely ill patient costs KRW 50,000; however, a critically ill patient will not get better. This will lead to another week on a mid-priced antibiotic for KRW 100,000, and the patient will not get better. Hence, there is no choice but to use an expensive antibiotic for a week, which costs KRW 300,000.

Looking at the math in this scenario, immediate treatment with expensive antibiotics takes a week and costs KRW 300,000 for medication. Starting with a low-cost antibiotic takes three weeks and costs KRW 450,000. What do you think? HIRA recommends the latter for doctors. The idea is to try a milder, cheaper antibiotic and progress to a more expensive antibiotic if the patient's condition does not improve.

However, can those sitting at a desk at the HIRA office determine a patient's condition? No. Even if they were in the clinic as non-doctors, they would be unable to make appropriate decisions about antibiotic selection. This should be the judgment and choice of the doctors treating the patient.

Treating a patient is not like pushing a button to get a drink from a vending machine. Patients are organisms with many variables, even for the same condition, such as co-existing conditions, weight, gender, and different responses to medications.

Lower Respiratory Tract Infections
Analytical Review Results

Provider information

Name of provider	Beautiful Breath Clinic
Provider number	11392851

Analysis review result

Thank you for your continued cooperation in promoting public health and advancing the health insurance system.

HIRA conducts topic-specific analytical reviews to support evidence-based and patient-centered care delivery using clinical and cost metrics developed through committees that include experts in healthcare for 11 topics, including hypertension, diabetes, asthma, chronic obstructive pulmonary disease, and lower respiratory tract infections.

By analyzing the data billed by providers, HIRA calculates the patient status by topic and the results of analytical indicators and guides providers to improve their patient care by comparing the analysis results with those obtained from other providers.

Here is a summary of your lower respiratory tract infection patient claims and metric results. We ask for your active interest and cooperation.

We would also like to remind you that you may be reviewed by an expert review committee comprising healthcare professionals if your metric results do not improve.

HIRA
Health Insurance Review & Assessment Service

A notification from HIRA to the Beautiful Breath Clinic about the results of an analysis of antibiotic prescriptions for lower respiratory tract disease, stating that the clinic will be subject to a review if no improvements are made.

Overall analysis results

● Lower respiratory tract infection metric results(your status)
- In the comprehensive assessment of the clinical and cost domain metrics in the lower respiratory tract infection metric review for the second half of 2023, your clinic is identified as being "in need of cost and quality management." We provide guidance on patient monitoring, follow-up, and testing for appropriate management of lower respiratory tract infections.

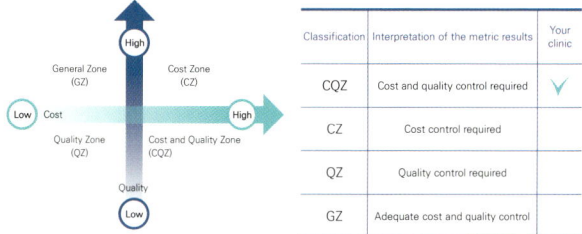

● Lower respiratory tract infections included in the analysis
- **(Claims)** Outpatient claims for patients aged 15 years and older with a principal or primary diagnosis of pneumonia (J13–J18), acute bronchitis (J20–J22), or chronic bronchitis (J40–J42) billed at an institution* subject to chronic obstructive pulmonary disease or asthma appropriateness assessment
  * 2021 8th Chronic Obstructive Pulmonary Disease or 2021 9th Asthma Appropriateness Criteria
- **(Period)** August 2023 – December 2023 Outpatient review decisions (second half of 2023)
- **(By beneficiary type)** Health Insurance, Medical Payments

● Outpatient Claims
- There were 6,677 outpatient claims for lower respiratory tract infections at your clinic for the second half of 2023, with 2,597 patients.

(Units: cases, people, cases, days, KRW)

Classification	Number of claims	Number of patients	Number of prescriptions	Visits per patient	Amount claimed
Total (outpatient)	10,754	3,881	9,274	3	1,177,019,772
Lower respiratory tract infections included in the analysis	6,677	2,597	5,623	3	626,795,562

The choice of antibiotics used by a pulmonologist to treat a patient is a significant medical decision. HIRA, which has no idea of the patient's condition, sends warnings that the Beautiful Breath Clinic must control costs and quality based on the high cost of our medications.

All areas of diagnosis and treatment are the domain of doctors.

Is that not why doctors take responsibility? If a patient's condition deteriorates, what responsibility can HIRA take? Can the National Health Insurance Service take responsibility for patients?

Responsibility should come with authority. Doctors have the duty, responsibility, and authority to take good care of their patients. Doctors are not concerned about the price of the medication prescribed to patients. Under the current system in which doctors must provide reimbursement for medications that they did not provide, is it not a serious issue for everyone to consider which doctors can provide the best medical treatment with only the patient in mind?

It was recently announced that clinics and hospitals will receive a 1.96% raise in 2025. In 2024, the base monthly income increased by 4.5% compared to that in 2023. The assumption is that the inflation rate in 2025 will also increase, not decrease. The government's attempts to save essential healthcare are a rallying cry.

I do not believe the fee for essential healthcare will ever catch up to its value. Who is going to step up to the plate to practice essential healthcare and save patients?

It is still 70% of the original cost even if it is increased by the general rate of inflation.

Despite the inflation rate of more than 4% per year, medical fees increase by less than 2% per year. In 5, 10, and 20 years, medical fees will be under 70% of the original cost. South Korea's essential healthcare system will collapse at an accelerated rate.

The DUR is a well-established system. Over the past 50 years, South Korea's healthcare system has become one of the best worldwide. I do not understand why they are trying to destroy our wonderful K-medicine. Who can protect and support the health of our children and future generations living in South Korea? I will age and become sick eventually. As a doctor, I am concerned about which doctor I would trust with my health.

A common perception is that education needs a plan for a hundred years. Why is it so? Education is crucial, as it shapes children and youth into the future leaders of our country.

The same is true for healthcare. Healthcare is more than merely treating patients. The country's future, people's health and happiness, and national security depend on it.

It is a matter that should not be decided based on the interests of a certain party and tactics or maneuvers for achieving them or "populist" policies. All the damage belongs to us and our descendants. Policymakers and politicians should not pass on debt burdens and responsibilities to future generations. It is time to face these problems and discuss them openly to address and solve them.

Our country's future will be in jeopardy if they continue to deceive the public by "playing possum."

05
Reality and illusion of symptoms

Symptoms are a patient's subjective perceptions of how they feel when they have a disease. Symptoms are medically categorized into five types.

First, episodic symptoms appear and then disappear completely. For example, symptoms of excruciating pain in the lower right abdomen due to acute appendicitis will likely disappear once the appendix is removed surgically.

Second, there are acute symptoms, which refer to those with rapid onset in patients. Most acute symptoms are caused by viral diseases such as a cold or flu and are easily treated. However, some conditions with acute symptoms require emergency treatment, such as myocardial infarction, cerebral hemorrhage, acute exacerbation of respiratory diseases, and pneumothorax.

Third, chronic symptoms occur, disappear, and reappear, resulting in repeated experiences of such symptoms. For example, bronchial asthma is characterized by a recurring cough and shortness of breath.

Fourth, recurrent symptoms are distinguished from chronic symptoms, which are characterized by short symptom-free periods and recur periodically. Recurrent symptoms are characterized by long periods without symptoms, do not recur as frequently as chronic symptoms, and are more responsive to treatment, such as a flare-up of depression, gout, or pneumonia. However, similar to a recurrence of cancer, when the underlying illness causing these symptoms resurfaces, it may not respond well to treatment and can be life-threatening.

Fifth, non-specific symptoms are not associated with a specific disease or anatomical organ. Coughing is a symptom of most respiratory illnesses, reflux esophagitis, or reflux laryngitis, making it a specific symptom. However, the symptoms of tiredness and helplessness are not specific to certain diseases. They can be caused by internal medical problems, such as thyroid, digestive, or cardiovascular problems, result from psychiatric problems, or be a precursor to various cancers. Occasionally, even healthy people can feel tired and lethargic, depending on how they function that day. Non-specific symptoms are important because it is impossible to pinpoint exactly what is wrong with the body.

In respiratory internal medicine, carefully recognizing which symptoms are real and which are not is essential. The main reason symptoms are important to patients is that they send them to the doctor. No patient goes to the hospital without any symptoms. The only time people visit a doctor without any symptoms is for a medical checkup.

Respiratory diseases bring patients to the hospital with symptoms such as cough, shortness of breath, chest pain, sputum, hemoptysis, and fever. Patients come to me without any of these symptoms but after a medical examination, with abnormal findings on a chest radiograph or chest CT scan.

Symptoms are tangible—they have a cause. Doctors should try to find the exact cause of a patient's symptoms and provide causal treatment. It is not uncommon for symptoms to be considered mild or treated without further investigation of the cause, especially if they have only been present for a short period. Doctors provide empirical care based on their clinical experience in symptomatic treatment.

No pulmonologist will recommend a chest CT or bronchoscopy for what appears to be a simple cold. Private clinics, especially t primary healthcare providers, tend to use symptomatic treatment often. Patients rarely visit university hospitals for a cough that has been frequent for only three days. They usually visit their neighborhood doctor, the patients' gateway to the healthcare system. Therefore, having a primary care doctor in one's neighborhood is extremely important, and it can be difficult to obtain a precise diagnosis at a local clinic. Patients often go to university hospitals when they have severe or long-standing symptoms or after having already been diagnosed with a suspected condition by their primary care doctor. Therefore, in terms of medical diagnosis, a primary healthcare provider may find it more difficult to diagnose an illness accurately. In terms of medical equipment, facility size, and staffing, university hospitals are far superior to private clinics. Currently, many available private specialty clinics have equipment and skills equivalent to those of university hospitals, making access to medical care more convenient for patients. One of the biggest medical challenges when examining and treating patients is the illusion of symptoms. An illusion is the appearance of something that is not present or when something is not what it appears to be. A 75-year-old man presented with a chronic cough that had been present for six months. A cough is defined as chronic when it persists for more than two months. Almost all patients with symptoms of a chronic cough go to the doctor. People visit the doctor when they have symptoms, and it would be strange not to see a doctor if one has been coughing for three months.

This patient had a chest radiograph performed at another hospital, which showed a tumor of approximately 8 cm in the left lung. The doctor who examined the patient determined that the tumor was caused by pulmonary tuberculosis and prescribed anti-tuberculosis medication. When the patient's cough did not improve after taking the tuberculosis medication, he came to the Beautiful Breath Clinic with a persistent cough.

After reviewing the patient's chest photograph, I explained that he would need a contrast-enhanced chest CT scan. A contrast-enhanced chest CT scan is performed when a tumor is suspected in the lungs. It differs from a low-dose chest CT scan that does not use a contrast medium. In diagnosing lung cancer, a contrast-enhanced chest CT scan is necessary to determine the presence of lymph node metastases, invasion of surrounding blood vessels by the tumor, and pleural metastases.

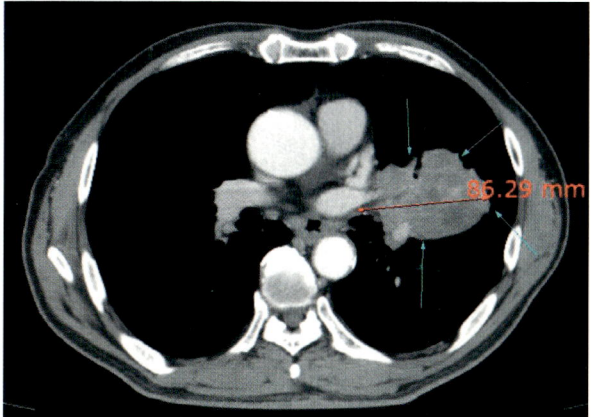

A contrast-enhanced chest CT showing a pulmonary mass
of approximately 8.6 cm in the left lung.

A contrast-enhanced chest CT scan does not confirm lung cancer. The diagnosis of lung cancer is made through a biopsy directly from the tumor. The method used to conduct this biopsy depends on the tumor's location. If it is close to the bronchus, a bronchoscopy is performed; if it is peripheral and far from the bronchus, a percutaneous needle aspiration biopsy is performed using a long needle from outside the lung. This patient underwent bronchoscopy with biopsy because the tumor was adjacent to the bronchi, and the biopsy confirmed lung cancer.

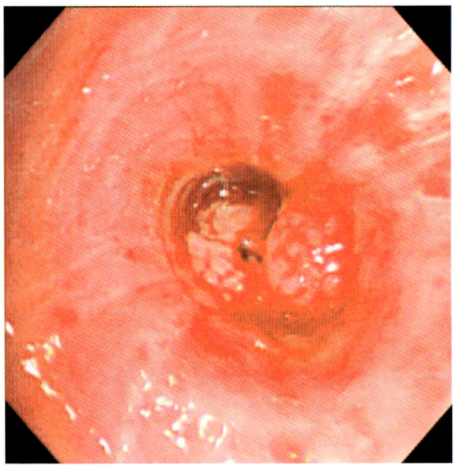

Bronchoscopy showing a mass blocking the left bronchus.

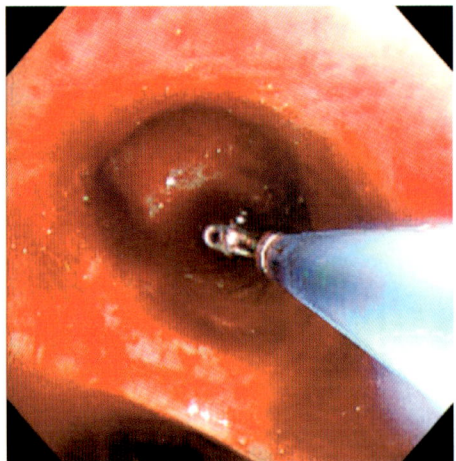

Bronchoscopic biopsy from a tumor confirming lung cancer.

This is a stark example of how dangerous false symptoms can be when treating patients, as well as a clear example of the importance of following proper protocol when diagnosing and treating tuberculosis rather than being fooled by the illusion of symptoms.

In principle, pulmonary tuberculosis should not be diagnosed and treated based on imaging tests alone. Tuberculosis is an infectious disease caused by Mycobacterium tuberculosis that enters the human body. The presence of Mycobacterium tuberculosis must be proven to diagnose pulmonary tuberculosis. The imaging findings of tuberculosis vary widely, as it may look typical or considerably different.

Caution is especially necessary when imaging findings of a pulmonary nodule or pulmonary cavity are present. Occasionally, there could be lung cancer; it is even more confusing for doctors. Indeed, lung cancer can show up with pulmonary tuberculosis. If a sputum test reveals Mycobacterium tuberculosis, almost all doctors would assume that it is pulmonary tuberculosis and would only treat it, would they not? The tuberculosis will be cured, but the patient will face a major consequence: missing the chance to treat the lung cancer in time.

Being a doctor, especially a pulmonologist, is difficult. The moment one releases the tension, the patient is lost.

A system exists for legal disputes that comprise courts of first instance, high courts, and the Supreme Court. Occasionally, a judgment in the first instance is overturned in the second. An accused defendant has more than one chance; however, a critically ill patient has only one chance. Losing that chance will either kill the patient or leave them with an irreversible, unrecoverable disability. Thus, a pulmonologist may not be the kind of person who is destined to savor a life of leisure.

When I wrote the book "I 'Need' You Whenever I 'Breathe'" six years ago, I thought I would choose the life of a pulmonologist if I were born again. I am a happy and blessed doctor; however, as I write this book now, if I were to reincarnate, I would not choose to become a doctor. I would not choose to be a pulmonologist again.
I want to be free of the pressure and gravity of being in charge of patients' lives. I want to live a "life with evenings," as has been popularly said. As a "life with evenings" is not simply about having

dinner at home, I realize that I have been missing out on life while being caught up in tension, and I would not want to live this way ever again.

Is happiness not found in the ordinary?
My life has been way too special. I do not mean to say that I have lived a good life. I am not saying that I have been blessed with a special talent. Emotions are contagious. I want to give my tired mind and body some rest after half a lifetime of struggling with the suffering of sick patients.

Chapter 5

Emotional outlet

Memory lane

Namhansanseong Fortress

Exit strategy

Try to go south by driving the chariot north

Perspectives on life and death

01
Emotional outlet

A 75-year-old man who came to the clinic had health anxiety—a somatoform disorder characterized by an abnormal concern and preoccupation with one's health because of a belief that one has a serious illness or a fear of contracting it. This patient could not live a normal life because he thought he had lung cancer whenever he caught a cold and coughed. When he first visited me, I did not realize he had health anxiety. When doctors see a patient for the first time, they ask, "What brings you here?"
When physicians examine a patient, they start by looking at the overall appearance of the patient. They observe the eyes, the complexion, the way of breathing, or any wounds on the body. Subsequently, they start asking the patient questions. Patients will describe their symptoms as a response to the question, "What is bothering you?"

This is the first step in the process of making a diagnosis. The 75-year-old man's symptoms included coughing, shortness of breath, chest pain, and blood in his sputum. All these symptoms would make a pulmonologist nervous. In particular, blood in the sputum suggested a strong case for testing. No doctor would ever hear of patients having blood in their sputum and give them a pill without any tests or tell them to "wait and see." Such a doctor would be either an unlicensed fraud or unstable.

After a detailed examination, including gathering information regarding whether he smoked, the time when the symptoms started, and the amount and color of the hemoptysis, I concluded that he needed to be evaluated. A generalized test cannot reveal many diseases of the lungs or bronchi. A low-dose chest CT and bronchoscopy were performed. His lungs were normal, and his bronchi showed chronic bronchitis. As bronchitis was identified as the cause of the hemoptysis, the patient was prescribed a therapeutic regimen with the explanation that the hemoptysis and cough were caused by chronic bronchitis.

Two weeks passed, and the 75-year-old patient returned to the clinic, complaining of the same symptoms. He said he had blood in his sputum, shortness of breath, and a cough. I explained that he had a complete checkup two weeks ago, and no further testing was necessary. Chronic bronchitis is a long-standing condition, and seeing blood in the sputum could be a concern. Nevertheless, as the cause was known, no further testing was needed.

However, this patient was adamant. He said he would like to have the bronchoscopy conducted again, assuming the earlier test may have been wrong.
I am an expert bronchoscopist.
Not all pulmonologists are proficient in bronchoscopy, but I happen to be a pulmonologist and an expert bronchoscopist. Therefore, I could not have accidentally missed bronchial or lung cancer, as the patient feared. The patient said he was uneasy about his persistent sputum and asked for another bronchoscopy. Normally, I would not give in to such unreasonable demands, but this patient was so insistent that I could not help but grant his request. The results were unchanged. There was no bronchial or lung cancer. He has since requested a bronchoscopy several times.

In this case, there could be only two possibilities. First, the patient could be experiencing a neuropsychiatric condition, a type of health anxiety. Second, the patient could be addicted to a sleep-inducing drug used during a bronchoscopy. It was determined that this patient had a severe case of health anxiety. Health anxiety is a condition in which a patient's anxiety, worry, and fear do not go away even when tests show they are not ill. They should seek neuropsychiatric care. However, the patient did not recognize his illness.

As these patients do not recognize their panic and fear as psychiatric problems, they do not seek a psychiatrist. They keep asking for more testing. If demanding does not work, they beg and plead. They try every trick in the book to get tested, fearing that if they are not tested, they will die of lung cancer.

Physicians are the ones who see patients, listen to their symptoms, and make the initial diagnosis. Patients do not discuss just their pain but talk about everything. Many patients unravel a treasure trove of stories beyond the reader's imagination.

The Korean health insurance system has structural problems that prevent doctors from listening to many of our patients' stories. Seeing 150 to 200 a day and performing tests and procedures in person will give few doctors the time to listen to all of their patients' stories. Doctors who see fewer than 30 patients a day may be able to do so, but an internal medicine practice that sees fewer than 30 patients a day cannot sustain itself and will go out of business. An internal medicine practice must see more than 60 patients a day to keep running.

This is not the doctor's fault but because the country has kept "medical fees" below their actual costs for over 50 years.

In South Korea, the term "emotional trash can" is popular among the Millennials and Gen Zs. Millennials and Gen Zs are often jointly referred to as the "MZ generation" in South Korea, which has suddenly become a popular concept through the media in the early 2020s. It is generally defined as referring to people born between 1981 and 2010, classified as early Millennials (1981-1988) and late Millennials (1989-1996). Millennials have been described as the first global generation and the first generation to grow up in the Internet age. This generation is generally characterized by increased use and familiarity with the Internet, mobile devices, and social media; thus, they are sometimes referred to as "digital natives."

An "emotional trash can" means an emotional outlet. It refers to a situation where a friend, acquaintance, or someone with whom you have some level of intimacy is constantly talking about their situation or circumstances and venting their feelings to you.

When you are the one listening to someone else's emotional outbursts, depressing stories, or struggles, you feel as if you are being used as their emotional outlet. While the MZ generation invented the term, older generations also experience being used as an emotional outlet by others. They could not define the phenomenon.

Patients using their doctors as emotional outlets is not uncommon. Patients say almost the same things every time they see me, such as "I'm sick," "I'm tired," "Why am I getting sick so fast?" "Why am I getting sick again?" "I've had tests, and why don't you know what's wrong with me?" "I've taken medication, and I'm not getting better." If each patient speaks ten words, when you see a hundred patients, you hear a thousand words. Patients have the right to speak up about their symptoms. Doctors are the ones who treat patients and have the duty to listen to them. Patients talk about many things unrelated to their illness.

A good doctor will listen, understand, and empathize with all of that. However, even the best doctors eventually feel hurt when they hear these negative comments from 100 or more patients daily for a year, ten years, twenty years, or more. People avoid being someone else's emotional outlet by dissociating from them as soon as they realize it. Nevertheless, doctors cannot dissociate themselves from their patients but can say no to excessive demands or unreasonable requests.

Doctors must control their emotions, even if it means being an emotional outlet for their patients. Doctors, especially those who provide essential healthcare, cannot afford to expend their energy to be an emotional outlet. Discussing an emotional outlet is too leisurely for doctors who strive to provide treatment and care that save patients' lives.

The reception desk next to the doctor's office could be a tough position serving as the clinic's emotional outlet.

02
Memory lane

Humans have been called the lord of all creations and rule the world because of their ability to remember and learn. The human brain has evolved to learn, remember, and apply new concepts.

God allowed the human brain to evolve, but He ensured that humans did not store every memory endlessly. If humans remembered everything they saw, heard, and experienced, they would be unable to live. Humans can live because of the ability to forget. Paradoxically, we survive because of our ability to remember, and we live because of our ability to forget.

We often have to take a trip down memory lane to bring back the small pieces of the memory.

A 76-year-old patient presented with hemoptysis, chest pain, and cough and was scheduled for bronchoscopy. Bronchoscopy is performed painlessly for the patient after administering an injection to induce sleep. Having performed countless bronchoscopies, I encountered a strange experience.

After a successful bronchoscopy for this patient, I was seeing another patient in my office. Subsequently, I heard a loud noise in the waiting room. When I found out what was going on, I realized that the patient who had just undergone a bronchoscopy was creating a scene and yelling at the staff. I escorted the excited patient into the doctor's office and had him sit in the examination chair. I asked him, "Dear patient, why are you yelling and fussing like that?"

"I didn't get my bronchoscopy," he responded.

What did he mean by that? He did not seem to be saying that he skipped the test but that he wanted a test and could not get it. What this patient meant by saying he did not get a bronchoscopy was that he thought I, the doctor, had not performed it.

This made me laugh. I explained that he had a successful bronchoscopy with a sleep-inducing medication. However, the patient insisted that he had no memory of it.

He was so assertive that he was angry and resentful, as if he had been cheated. I explained again, showing him a picture of his bronchoscopy. Bronchoscopic images are displayed with the date and time of the test, as well as the patient's name and registration number. As bronchoscopy is an extremely important test, the time is displayed to the nearest minute and second.

Even when I showed him the records, he did not believe me. He ended up crossing a line that should not have been crossed. He threatened to sue me for damages, insisting that he paid for a bronchoscopy and did not get it. His wife, who came with him as a guardian, also spoke up. Sometimes, it is the opposite. However, it was my first time encountering someone insisting they did not get a bronchoscopy. It is not uncommon for a patient to report that they had an endoscopy under sedation and felt pain without falling completely asleep.

I can empathize with their concerns. I understand that the purpose of having a bronchoscopy done while asleep is to have the test performed without pain or distress, which is why the patient pays more. However, I have never encountered a patient who was so comfortable with it that he denied having it done. This meant that he had a considerably good sleep bronchoscopy.

Nonetheless, the patient did not acknowledge that he had undergone the procedure.

Earlier, I mentioned the memory lane. This man went down memory lane but found not even a piece of the memory, which was rather extraordinary. Would a normal person not recognize when they see a picture and hear an explanation, even if they have no memory of being tested?

What could have caused the patient's severe distrust? I have mentioned

many times that trust between a patient and their doctor is a significant part of diagnosing and treating illnesses.
The trust between patient and doctor is called a rapport in medical jargon. "Rapport" is a French word that refers to a relationship of mutual trust that develops between people. In the medical context, the term is used specifically to express a "relationship of trust" between a doctor and a patient. Despite my detailed explanation, the patient did not trust my words and was fixated on not remembering being tested. My rapport with this patient had already been broken.

I could not accommodate the demands of the patient and his guardian. The test was performed accurately, and the detailed results would be available in a week. The patient left with threats to sue me. Doctors who specialize in essential healthcare and deal with patients' lives hear this all the time. What is the dictionary definition of suing?

Suing is an expression of the intent of a victim of a crime, or someone with a specific relationship to the victim, to report the crime to law enforcement and seek punishment for the perpetrator. Simply reporting a crime to law enforcement without seeking to punish the perpetrator is not considered suing. The difference between suing and reporting is that reporting is conducted by a third party, who is not the person with the right to request a lawsuit, by filing out a crime report with an investigative agency and seeking punishment for the perpetrator. Suing is an expression of a desire for punishment; therefore, one must have the power to file a lawsuit.

You can imagine the stress on doctors up to this point. Suing requires a criminal offense; what did the doctor do?
In this patient's case, filing a lawsuit would not even be possible in the first place. In my years of diagnosing and treating critically ill respiratory patients, I have heard the word "sue" numerous times.
The number of patients who have threatened to sue is less than 0.001% of the total population of patients I have treated. You might think that one patient out of a thousand is not a big deal. However, the

Beautiful Breath Clinic has over 110,000 registered patients, and I have had over 2 million visits. Statistically, 0.001% of 110,000 is a hundred, and 0.001% of two million is over two thousand. If we are strict and only consider the number of registered patients, imagine being sued by 100 patients.

Which doctor would be willing to undergo this stress to provide essential healthcare? I can recall a dozen cases where I have been sued. In one case, I appeared in court, took the witness oath, sat on the witness stand, and answered the judge's questions. The case was in litigation for five years.

Doctors only know what doctors do. So do I. They are often extremely naïve in the outside world. As a medical student, I had no idea how the world worked. Except for the five hours I was asleep, I spent my days in lecture halls and libraries.
I did not know much about the 1988 Seoul Olympics, the World Cup, or the election of President Kim Young-sam, which ushered in the first civilian government in South Korea. I studied tirelessly to become the best doctor I could be for the patients I would someday meet and treat. I was not the only one who had such a medical school experience.
While a few medical students were interested in the mission of the times, such as social engagement and pro-democracy movements, and others were happy to play, I was unusually immersed in the academic side of medicine. I chose my specialty when the best interns could choose to specialize in internal medicine, and many doctors chose essential healthcare.

It was a time when you could feel the true essence of being a doctor. Over the course of 30 long years, essential healthcare has been slowly dying. One reason is that the work is much harder and less rewarding than that of an aesthetic doctor.
The lack of compensation and the violent behavior and accusations by some insensitive patients and their guardians are extremely stressful. This physically demanding, economically unrewarding, and mentally

draining state of being has lasted for 30 years.

Is the collapse of essential healthcare a foregone conclusion?

Association is not the same as causality; it is the quality or characteristic by which things or phenomena have a certain relationship. It can also be described as relevance or continuity. Association analysis is an analytical method for determining the relationship between variables based on a measure of the data collected from the population under investigation. It is inappropriate to explain the collapse of essential care by association.

Causality is the property that if there is a cause, there will always be an effect. It refers to a cause-and-effect relationship between two or more things.

In The Theory of Human Intellect, the philosopher John Locke described causality as the productive relationship of ideas. In particular, the thing that produces an idea is called a cause, and the thing that it produces is called an effect. Causality is understood as the mind's construct of the relationship between ideas, and these ideas are highly psychologically influenced.

The collapse of essential healthcare is due to doctors perceiving it as challenging. The cause stems from the national healthcare system, a product of the era where authority began fading. Without accurate analysis and solutions, the healthcare system in South Korea may encounter even stranger and more catastrophic consequences in 2024. Ultimately, K-medicine, South Korea's fastest, most accurate, and most economical healthcare option, could become a thing of the past.

03
Namhansanseong Fortress

Namhansanseong Fortress is located in Namhansanseong-myeon, Gwangju-si, Gyeonggi-do, South Korea. It is commonly known as a mountain fortress built to defend Hanyang, the capital of the Joseon Dynasty, along with Bukhansanseong Fortress. However, recent excavations have confirmed the remains of walls and buildings from the mid-8th century, suggesting it is the former site of Shilla's Jujangseong Fortress. It was an important "base fortress" where special warehouses were installed to store military supplies; during the Joseon Dynasty, it was a typical mountain fortress with inner and outer walls.

I am a resident of Jamsil, Songpa-gu. Jamsil is a short distance away from Namhansanseong Fortress, which can be reached by car in approximately 15 minutes. I lived in Jamsil for 20 years and had never been to Namhansanseong Fortress.

Namhansanseong Fortress is a considerably famous mountain fortress, and I have watched a movie named after it. Most people in South Korea are probably familiar with Namhansanseong Fortress. I eventually went to Namhansanseong Fortress by chance.

The first time I visited Namhansanseong Fortress, I was in for a surprise. I remember it was the end of a warm spring day, and the sky was clear. On the way there, the natural scenery outside the car window was amazing.

Until I visited Namhansanseong Fortress, I assumed it would be similar to Haengjusanseong Fortress, which I had visited before. I made this assumption because I thought both sites were in the same category of mountain fortress. This was a complete illusion. The mountains were lush and green with valleys, and their shape stretching from east to west and north to south was like a natural fortress.

Even without any knowledge of military history, I could understand the importance of Namhansanseong Fortress as a military base. On the way up to Namhansanseong Fortress, there were many restaurants, cafes, and bakeries. I walked into a restaurant to eat.

I ate homemade tofu and mountain vegetable bibimbap. When I was younger, I loved tofu, soybean paste stew, and rich soybean paste stew. When I reached my 40s, I began to have a difficult time eating beans, tofu, and soybean paste stew because of my irritable bowel syndrome. As my body struggled, I could no longer enjoy my favorite foods and stayed away from them.

However, in that restaurant in Namhansanseong Fortress, I could not resist. I would rather have just eaten and endured the gas. I tasted tofu for the first time in a long while; nonetheless, it was not only the food that made it an unforgettable day.

I thought about my life while enjoying the beautiful scenery. Sleepless nights and early mornings at the hospital. I start seeing patients two hours earlier than other clinics. After treating various patients including those who are critically ill, my body is exhausted, and my mind is in a state of extreme fatigue.

Some patients have been coughing for more than two months, some have been coughing for more than 10 years, and some are short of breath. Further, some patients have chest pain, some are coughing up blood, some have excessive sputum to breathe, and some others are on portable oxygen. Moreover, some patients' conditions have deteriorated despite treatment at other hospitals, some have a high fever, and some come in for bronchoscopy because they suspect lung cancer.

Patients come to me from all over the country with a wide variety of symptoms.

Patients who come to us with respiratory symptoms have been to multiple hospitals, including university hospitals. These patients are desperate and see us as their "last hope."

My day is full of tension as I treat patients who come to me thinking of the Beautiful Breath Clinic as their last resort. I cannot think at a leisurely pace, and the sense of urgency of not knowing when a patient will come in with an emergency keeps me on my toes throughout my day at the clinic. My nervousness and sensitivity while performing bronchoscopy are unimaginable. You would not know it if you did not experience it. Patients or guardians may be unaware of this and need not know it.

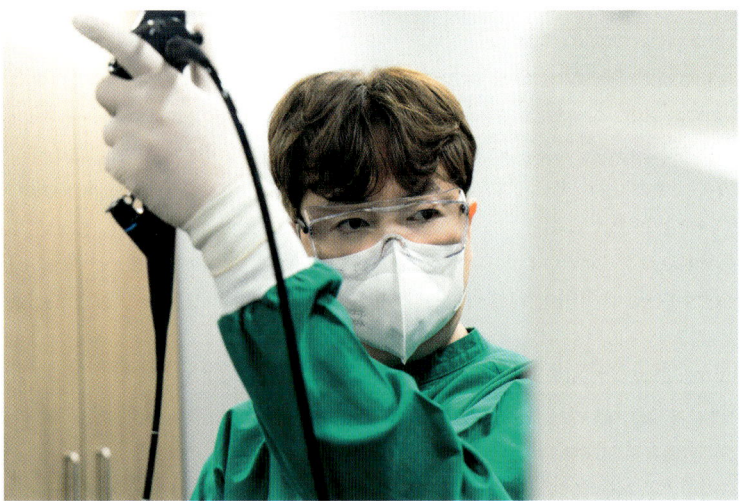

The look in Dr. SEONGLIM JIN's eyes during a bronchoscopy.
It is full of tension.

What makes a doctor a doctor? Regardless of how stressful or high-risk a test or procedure is, doctors need not share those feelings with their patients, and patients need not know about them. Understandably, patients care more about their symptoms and want to be cured of their illnesses. Doctors know the gravity of the pressure they feel when performing a procedure like a bronchoscopy. Those days added up to 23 years. Over time, I developed a habit of looking at my day negatively and feeling unhappy.

I started comparing my life to that of other doctors and thinking of the pain I feel when I see a critically ill patient as some sort of "elitism." I have done what I am supposed to do and have chosen to do.
It was not until I saw the lush greenery of Namhanshanseong Fortress that I felt ashamed of thinking as if someone had forced me into a "crucible of pain." Enlightenment can come slowly, but on that day, I realized that enlightenment can also happen in an instant, like a lightning strike. It was a life-changing moment, a shift in perception.

Man is a social animal. The timeless words of the ancient Greek philosopher Aristotle resonate with us today, more than 2,000 years later, because social bonds—the essence of human nature—are weakening. According to the Ministry of Public Administration and Safety, 40.1% of the nation's registered households are "one-person households," followed by "two-person households" at 23.8%. Combined, "one- and two-person households" represent 63.9% of all households in South Korea.

This surge in "one-person households" has led to social issues such as loneliness and lonely death. According to a 2018 report by the Korea Institute for Health and Social Affairs (KIHASA), "Social Relationships of Young Single-Person Households," young single-person households spend an average of only five minutes a day with their families.

However, the average amount of time they spend interacting with non-family members is 47 minutes. According to a 2019 Statistics Korea survey, South Korea's social isolation rate is 27.7%, which is well above the OECD average of 10%.

Why is loneliness a health risk for humans?
At its 125th annual conference in the United States in 2017, the American Psychiatric Association warned that loneliness and social

isolation may pose a greater threat to public health than obesity as a cause of chronic disease. "Social connection with others is a basic human need, crucial to our well-being and survival," said Julianne Holt-Lunstad, a professor of psychiatry at Brigham Young University in the United States, adding that children who grow up with little human contact suffer from stunted physical and emotional development and sometimes even death.

An analysis of two large studies presented by the professor showed strong evidence that social isolation and loneliness threaten human health. He argued that modern society is facing a "loneliness epidemic." Chronic respiratory disease is common in older adults due to the nature of the disease. Twenty years ago, when seeing chronic respiratory patients, if there was any indication that their condition was likely to progress and get worse, they were advised to bring their guardians with them, and most of them did.

Now, 20 years later, when I tell patients to bring a guardian, nine out of ten say they do not have one, even when they do—they live alone, and their children are too busy to come to the clinic with them.

It is unhealthy for even healthy people to live alone. It is extremely dangerous for anyone, let alone a sick person, especially those with respiratory conditions who may experience shortness of breath and sudden emergencies. I feel sad and sorry for them. Being short of breath and coughing all night causes unspeakable pain and sorrow for patients, and how fearful they must be when they are alone with no one to care for them.

Despite the day full of pain and the hourly fears and aches that come along, severe respiratory patients come to see me with hope. Regardless of how difficult and challenging my life is, it does not even compare to the anguish and struggle of those with critical respiratory disease.

This is why I have been practicing medicine for 30 years and why I cannot let go of the mission of "essential healthcare" in South Korea.

04
Exit strategy

An "exit strategy" is a means of getting out of a bad situation. The term originally referred to the retreat of an army that had completed its mission. However, in economics, it refers to the reversal of economic policy. When used in business terminology, it refers to a strategy that minimizes economic losses.

An exit strategy is also important for interpersonal relationships—especially intimate ones. The human mind is a fickle thing, and what is good in the morning can be bad in the evening. There is a saying that a woman is a weathercock, but all humans are like weathercocks. Consistency and integrity are vital when working or engaging in economic activities while socializing with others. Most people live their lives like that.

Not just women; we are all weathercocks.

What goes up must come down. An evil may sometimes turn out to be a blessing in disguise There is an old story of an old man and his running horse.
Let me tell you the full story.
An old man lived in a border province of China. One day, the old man's horse escaped across the border into barbarian territory. When his neighbors offered words of comfort, the old man seemed unconcerned, saying, "Who knows, this may turn out to be a blessing in disguise." One day, a few months later, the runaway horse returned with a female horse. "It's just as you said," the neighbors celebrated.

However, the old man was not pleased, saying, "Who knows, this may turn out to be an evil in disguise?" A few days later, the old man's son fell off the horse while riding it and broke his leg. When the neighbors tried to comfort him again, the old man said, "This may be a blessing in disguise," without changing his expression. Soon after, the barbarians from the north invaded. The country issued conscription, forcing all young men to go to war. Nevertheless, the old man's son did not have to go to war because he had a broken leg.
This story is what a blessing in disguise is all about. As the old man in the border province said, what appeared to be a blessing could end up an evil, and what appeared to be an evil could end up a blessing. We never know how things will turn out at the end of the day. You should not be too concerned with the outcome of what is happening in front of you.
This is similar to the concept of an exit strategy. There is no medical term for an exit strategy. Nevertheless, my long experience as a pulmonologist has taught me that treating disease also requires an exit strategy. This is especially necessary for patients who have been smoking for many years.
After spending so much time as a smoker, patients may think, "What's the point of quitting now?" This is a complete illusion and a false idea. Smoking is one of the worst habits that harm human health and causes many respiratory diseases.

Smoking itself is a disease and a serious one at that. We could spend a year listing and explaining the diseases smoking can cause. When talking about lung cancer alone, with which many people are familiar, the story is endless.

A 76-year-old patient visited the beautiful breath clinic with hemoptysis. There is a habitual question that I ask every patient who comes in with respiratory symptoms, regardless of age and gender. I ask this question to men, women, the young, and the old. I always ask this question to those aged 15 or older. "Do you smoke?" This patient had been smoking for a whopping 60 years. Smoking a pack of cigarettes a day for 60 years is medically referred to as 60 pack-years of "smoking history."

The risk of developing lung cancer is more than 15 times higher for those with a smoking history of 30 pack-years or more than for nonsmokers. This patient smoked two packs of cigarettes a day for 60 years. With a smoking history of 120 pack-years, the risk of developing lung cancer increases hundreds of times. A doctor should not be practicing medicine if they do not recommend and order chest radiography when a smoker with a 120-pack-year smoking history presents with symptoms of hemoptysis.

As a pulmonologist, I would probably say that a chest CT is required even if a simple chest x-ray comes back normal. If the low-dose chest CT scan comes back normal, I would insist on a contrast-enhanced chest CT scan.

Even if a contrast-enhanced chest CT scan comes back normal, I would try to convince the patient to have a bronchoscopy. Low-dose chest CT is currently the standard method for diagnosing early lung cancer, but a normal low-dose chest CT result does not mean that lung cancer is 100% absent. What does it mean then? University hospitals and screening centers are ordering low-dose chest CTs for early lung cancer diagnosis. However, a low-dose chest CT may fail to find lung cancer.

Low-dose chest CT is superior to simple chest radiographs and reduces deaths from lung cancer by 20% compared to screening with a simple chest radiograph alone. Therefore, it has become accepted wisdom in the medical community following the publication of large-scale studies. Nevertheless, even a low-dose chest CT scan is not a perfect test.

The human lung has an anatomical organ called a pulmonary hilum on each side. This is where the blood vessels are clustered. If a cancerous mass develops in the pulmonary hilum area, a low-dose chest CT scan may not be able to detect it. This is a trap no doctor can escape.

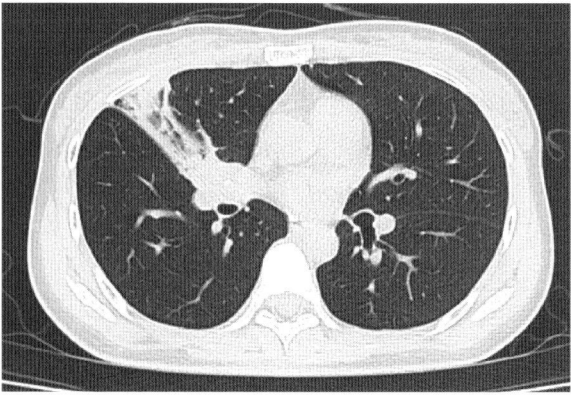

Low-dose chest CT: White shading in the lower lobe of the right lung read as pneumonia. The tumor is not visible in the right pulmonary hilum area because of the clustering of blood vessels.

Although this is a clear case of misdiagnosis, the doctor cannot be held medically or legally liable. If the doctor or hospital were to be held liable in such a case, a contrast-enhanced chest CT scan would be required for all people being screened to ensure early detection of lung cancer. Some may say, "What if we all just get a contrast-enhanced chest CT scan?" Nonetheless, when trying to detect a condition early for screening purposes, it is important to consider the cost-benefit and effectiveness of the test and whether it poses a risk to healthy people.

A contrast-enhanced chest CT scan is an essential test for staging and diagnosing lung cancer but carries the risk of radiation exposure and, in severe cases, a potentially life-threatening allergic reaction to the contrast medium injections.

Thus, large-scale testing of healthy people is not generally accepted. However, approaching it as an exit strategy, a contrast chest CT may be performed on an individualized basis for those at high risk of developing lung cancer. Furthermore, a contrast chest CT should be performed if a simple chest X-ray has already shown evidence of a tumor. Bronchoscopy is also a necessary test. Lung cancer is broadly categorized into small cell carcinoma and non-small cell carcinoma, with completely different treatment approaches, prognoses, and drug options.

The patient was tested and found to have lung cancer. As he has been diagnosed with lung cancer anyway, why bother quitting smoking?

Quitting smoking is absolutely necessary. It is not done until it is done, and the moment you think it is late may be the earliest moment. Modern lung cancer treatment has advanced considerably, and a diagnosis of lung cancer is no longer the death sentence. This goes without saying, especially if it is an operable lung cancer, and the patient is a candidate for targeted anti-cancer drug therapy or immunotherapy.

An integral part of the treatment of lung cancer is to stop smoking. Quitting smoking is important for the treatment of lung cancer.

It is the first step in treating COPD, one of the most common respiratory diseases caused by smoking. An exit strategy is the beginning of the treatment. An exit strategy is no longer merely a military concept or an economics term but a crucial medical strategy.

05
Try to go south by driving the chariot north

"Try to go south by driving the chariot north" is an old proverb. It is a metaphor for a contradiction of one's mind and actions or a contradiction of things.
It is often quoted in human relationships or judgments of right and wrong. It is also a concept to keep in mind when treating patients. A patient's symptoms often contradict a hidden condition, and the medication selected to treat the patient may contradict the coexisting condition.
A woman in her early 50s came in out of breath. After being diagnosed with asthma at another hospital and taking steroids, long-acting bronchodilator inhalers, short-acting bronchodilator inhalers, and oral bronchodilators, her breathing became more difficult. She came to the Beautiful Breath Clinic after being introduced by an acquaintance.

All patients who present with shortness of breath have their oxygen saturation checked immediately at the reception desk. She had an oxygen saturation of 78%. The receptionist immediately realized it was an emergency and notified the doctor's office, regardless of the waiting list of patients. An oxygen saturation of 78% suggests a critical respiratory condition.

The patient was short of breath, had an oxygen saturation of 78% (normal oxygen saturation: 98-99%), and was being treated for asthma. The first thing I had to do was listen to the patient's breathing. I used a stethoscope to listen to the sounds of the patient's lungs and bronchi.

I could hear wheezing sounds indicating severe asthma symptoms, as well as crackling sounds suggesting inflammation of the alveoli. The patient's face was pale, her breathing was labored, and she complained of chest tightness.

An emergency may call for immediate first aid measures before proceeding to an examination. In this patient, acute exacerbation of bronchial asthma was evident, and tests could be performed after emergency injection treatment.

In the case of an acute asthma attack, acute exacerbation of COPD, acute exacerbation of pulmonary fibrosis, sepsis, pneumonia, severe pneumonia with altered consciousness, or acute exacerbation of acute respiratory dysfunction syndrome (ARDS), therapeutic injections may be given quickly because of insufficient time to take photographs and perform blood tests.

As I was about to give the patient oxygen and the systemic high-dose steroids and short-acting bronchodilators used in acute exacerbations of bronchial asthma, another potential condition flashed across my mind.

The chest tightness and chest pain among the patient's symptoms were clues. An acute exacerbation of bronchial asthma is characterized by shortness of breath due to the contraction of bronchial smooth muscle after exposure to a cold or flu of any cause. Therefore, it could be accompanied by chest pain. However, in my clinical experience, patients complaining of chest pain during an exacerbation of acute asthma is rare. Patients tend to express the most distressing symptoms first. An acute exacerbation of bronchial asthma is characterized by shortness of breath, where breathing in is so difficult that the patient speaks more emphatically about the difficulty of breathing. Nevertheless, the initial complaints of this patient were chest tightness and shortness of breath.

The chest tightness really caught my attention.

I stopped the emergency injection treatment before it started and ordered an immediate electrocardiogram and chest radiography first.

It was just before the injection was to be administered intravenously. The clinical pathologist and radiologist acted quickly, and the tests were completed in less than two minutes. The results sent chills down my spine. I immediately called 911 for an ambulance.

The patient had an acute exacerbation of bronchial asthma, which was also accompanied by a myocardial infarction. An acute exacerbation of bronchial asthma is a serious condition and requires immediate unblocking of the narrowed bronchi to survive. Myocardial infarction is a critical condition in which the blood vessels in the heart become blocked, causing necrosis and death of the heart muscle.

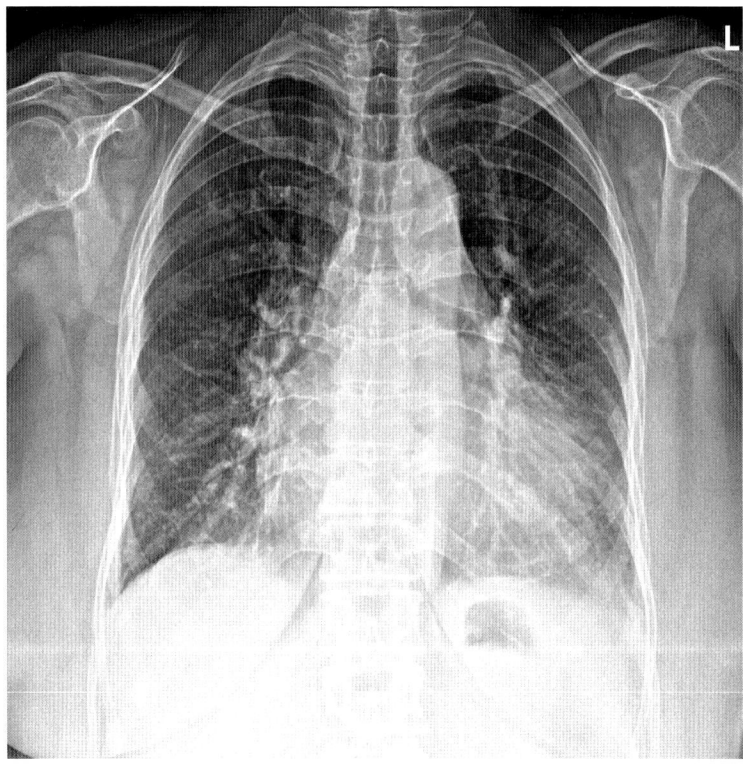

A photograph of a stretched heart from a myocardial infarction.

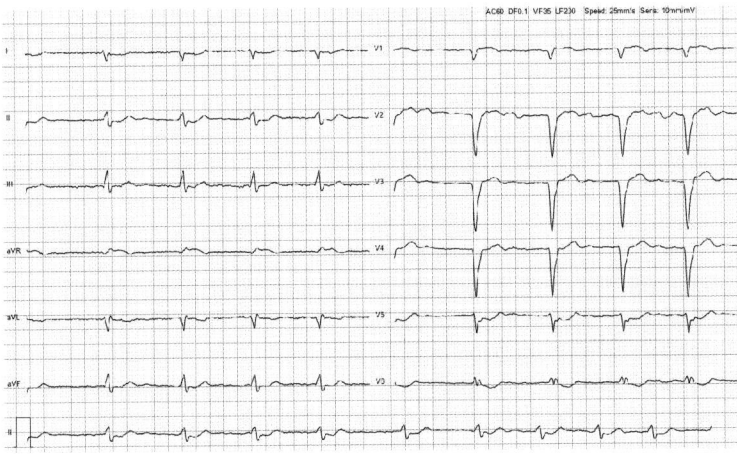

Electrocardiogram: V1-V4 chest deep Q-wave ST-segment elevation with evidence of acute myocardial infarction.

Both are critical conditions, but myocardial infarction has a higher mortality rate. Myocardial infarction should be treated first before treating the acute exacerbation of bronchial asthma.

If the patient's myocardial infarction had not been detected sooner, and she had been given high doses of systemic steroids and bronchodilators intravenously to treat acute exacerbations of asthma, she could have died immediately.

The first-line treatment for myocardial infarction involves balloon dilation of the blocked blood vessels in the heart and placement of a cardiac stent. Additionally, medications called "beta blockers" are prescribed to reduce fatigue in the heart muscle. Beta2-agonists, which are used for acute exacerbations of bronchial asthma, make the heart work harder and should not be used in patients with myocardial infarction.

It was a close call. What about the acute exacerbation of bronchial asthma? The blockage of the breathing passageway must be addressed. As inhaled bronchodilators do not put much strain on the heart, inhaled short-acting bronchodilators and inhaled steroids can be used to loosen the smooth muscle of the blocked bronchi.

The findings were just like "trying to go south by driving the chariot north." Contradictory treatments were being given in a contradictory situation.

A specialist cannot provide accurate treatment based on medical knowledge alone. A competent clinician is expected to apply their medical knowledge appropriately. In addition to a thorough and in-depth knowledge of respiratory diseases, a pulmonologist should have extensive knowledge and clinical experience in cardiology. The lungs and heart are closely related, and patients with lung disease often have heart disease as well.

Moreover, a keen sense of recognizing patients' "little cries" is essential. This is why pulmonologists are not destined to become comfortable in their practice and let their guard down. I have to be on my toes with all my senses on high alert while seeing my patients. That is the only way to save them.

Sensitivity and agility, reflexive judgment and execution in various emergencies, and compassion for critically ill patients have built the foundation of the Beautiful Breath Clinic today. However, there is another important fact. The equipment at the Beautiful Breath Clinic is actually better than that found in a university hospital. Here are simple chest radiographs from the Beautiful Breath Clinic and a university hospital.

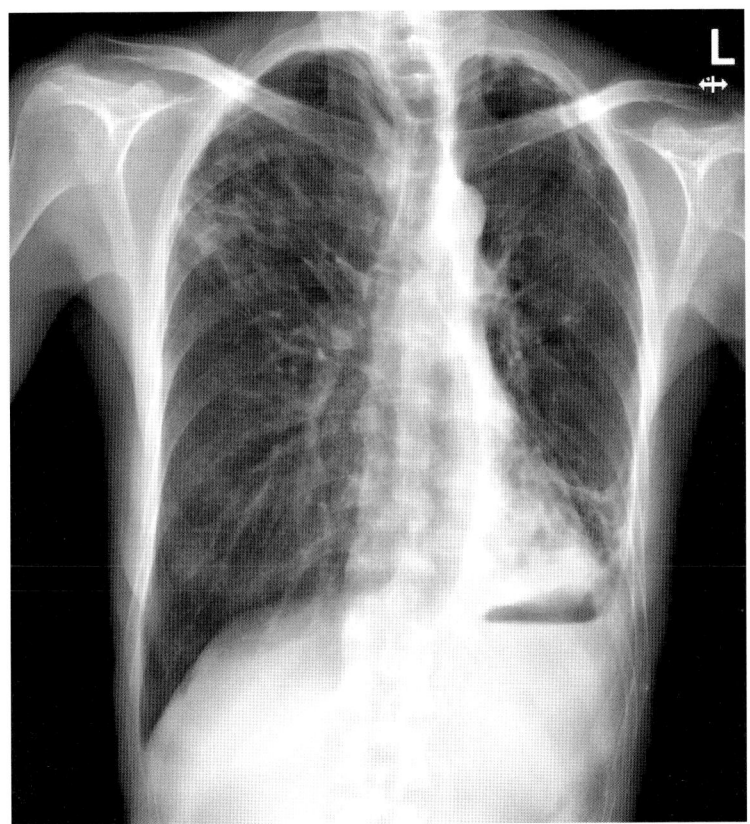

Simple chest radiograph from a university hospital:
A lesion appears white on the right.
The overall sharpness is too low to see the lesion in detail.

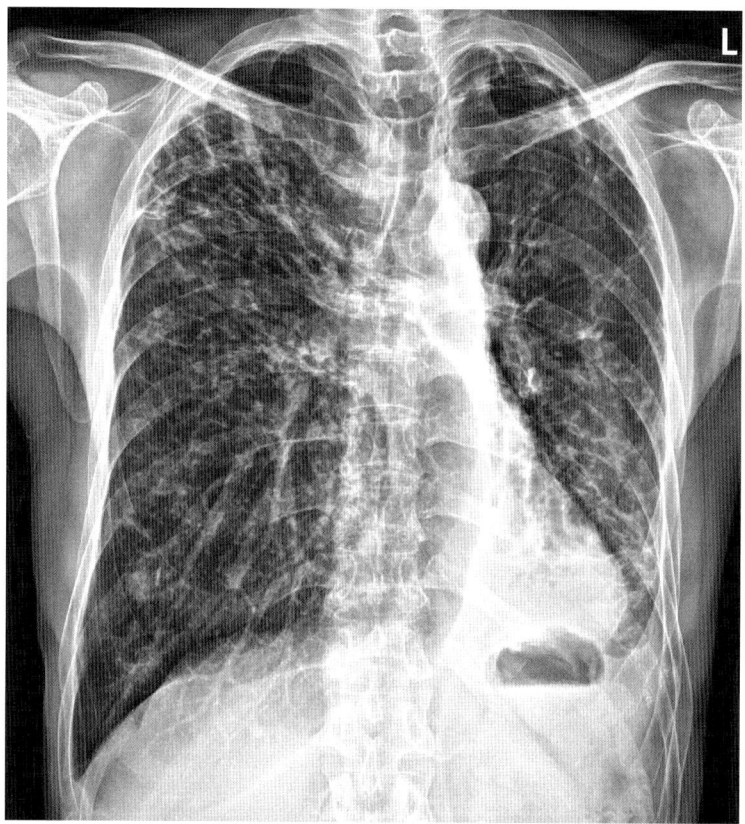

Simple chest radiograph from the Beautiful Breath Clinic. The clarity of the image is considerably good, where the abnormalities resemble white snowflakes across both lungs rather than just the upper lobe of the right lung.

06
Perspectives on life and death

What do you think life is? How about "death?"
After being a doctor for 30 years, I have seen more deaths than most people who are not doctors. However, there is no need to compare myself to non-doctors. Even among doctors in the same profession, I have experienced more patient deaths than others. A pulmonologist is a doctor who specializes in treating the lungs and bronchi, which are essential organs for human survival. The lungs are with us from our first breath as a newborn baby to our last moment of life.

The human brain can be deprived of oxygen for as little as four minutes before brain cells die. Along with the heart, the lungs play an important role in supplying oxygen and necessary nutrients to the brain. Respiratory diseases are common in the elderly, but it is true the other way around. The elderly have respiratory problems, and whether it is the natural process of aging or dying of illness, they will eventually stop breathing.
In addition to internal respiratory diseases, if a patient has a problem after a surgical procedure, a pulmonologist will address it. Furthermore, besides internal medicine intensive care units, surgical intensive care units are the workplace of pulmonologists. It is no coincidence that the doctors in charge of intensive care units are most often pulmonologists.
This is not unique to South Korea. In modern medicine, the specialist in charge of critical care medicine is a pulmonologist. Pulmonologists often see patients' pain and suffering as well as their deaths. During the first year of my pulmonology residency, I wrote ten death certificates

a day.

The average person does not experience death often. One may experience the death of a few loved ones. which is considerably different from the experience of seeing others die in the course of one's work. The emotions are incomparable.
Nonetheless, from a professional standpoint, seeing death so frequently can be extremely traumatizing. Death is inevitable for everyone. From the moment of birth, every human being is on a path toward death.

It is the life of a person to come and go empty-handed, and we cannot let go of greed as if we were eternal beings. Those who have money scramble to make more money, and those who seek honor strive to achieve greater honor.

Why is human history a history of warfare? Is it not human nature to want more?
Doctors who work in critical healthcare may have a pessimistic view of death. However, there is a flip side. Knowing that life is finite and what the outcome of the disease will be, they make the best of their lives and recognize the value of good health.

Most essential healthcare doctors know the value of good health. Nevertheless, they often fail to take good care of themselves because they cannot avoid being under extreme stress. The pressure of being responsible for a person's life is something no one can understand without experiencing it first. This pressure is a natural consequence of doctors' sense of responsibility to their patients, as well as to protect themselves.

Answering the question of what is the meaning of life generally constitutes a philosophical topic addressing the purpose and meaning of existence. Historically, this question has been the subject of philosophical, scientific, theological, and metaphysical consideration, and many answers have been proposed based on different cultures and ideas.

The scientific exploration of life has provided numerous insights—from happiness in life to anxiety about death. The study of life and reality, such as the Big Bang theory of the universe, the origin of life, and evolution, and the study of objective factors that correlate with the subjective experience of happiness have been conducted in various ways.

Neuroscience explains reward, joy, and motivation in terms of neurotransmitter activity in the limbic system. Believing that the meaning of life is to maximize pleasure and make life easier in general, normative predictions can be made about how to act to achieve this. Similarly, ethical scientists advocate the science of morality, the empirical pursuit of the flourishing of conscious creatures.

My perspective on life as a pulmonologist is that human life is precious. This idea comes from the experience of seeing how painful life is for patients.

The lives of respiratory patients are heartbreaking to witness. The depth of their pain is immeasurable. How dare I put such pain and suffering into words? This is why a person's life is so precious; one must be thankful for every day.

"What will it profit a man if he gains the whole world, yet forfeits his soul?" (Mark 8:36) is a biblical quote that runs through human history and destiny. No philosophical questions or answers can outweigh the value of this phrase.

Although life is filled with different emotions, we do not particularly want anger and sadness. Our hearts seek joy and happiness. If you lose your health, you lose everything. Life hurts when you lose your relaxed, beautiful breathing. Pain is also a part of life, but you know it when you experience it.

The fear of death comes in fleeting moments. Everyone dies, and the pain of dying does not last long. If the shadow of indescribable pain dominates one's existence and haunts the later years of one's life, it is not a momentary pain but a present and future pain.

Therefore, we should always strive to keep our lungs healthy. The government is responsible for taking care of respiratory patients. The government's raison d'être is to protect people's health and property. The health of the people is more precious and valuable than property and wealth.

Pulmonologists cannot create systems and funds. Pulmonologists are only doctors who treat individual patients with respiratory conditions. Is it not the government's responsibility to understand the plight and suffering of respiratory patients and provide a new future for them?

The general manager, who graduated from one of the best universities in South Korea, is intelligent and kind.

Managers, Lee Won-hee and Lee Mi-young who have worked with me for 19 years.

Chapter 6

One last thing to say to patients before closing the book:
a good doctor is a doctor who has just one more thought

One last thing to say to patients before closing the book:

a good doctor is a doctor who has just one more thought

What do you think makes a good doctor?

Would one become a good doctor after graduating from Seoul National University College of Medicine? If the rank of a medical school could determine the quality of a doctor, all graduates of Seoul National University College of Medicine would be great doctors, and graduates of Harvard Medical School in the United States would be even greater doctors.

Being a good doctor has nothing to do with doing well on college admissions.

Without saying "good doctor," an average doctor also has nothing to do with the college admissions. The grades necessary to enter a college are nothing more than what they are. Especially in the current university admissions system, where math is overwhelmingly dominant, it is not relevant to the problems of medicine.

As mentioned earlier, medicine is close to the humanities while being in the domain of natural sciences, as it deals with patients who are humans. It is not dealing with a broken thing but a sick person. The ability to understand people and empathize with their pain cannot be learned.

People are born with it. This is what we call personality.

Personality cannot be quantified. Consequently, medical students are selected based on grades. A great brain does not imply a great personality. Good brains are important to the advancement of medicine, but they are not always necessary to treat patients.

The most important thing to have when treating patients is an attitude

of "think of one more thing and try one more thing."
A 67-year-old woman came to the Beautiful Breath Clinic with shortness of breath, cough, and sputum that had continued for nine months. This patient was from Busan, South Korea, where she had been to several neighborhood clinics. Moreover, she has been to secondary healthcare institutions and university hospitals.
The diagnosis was bronchial asthma. Ninety percent of patients who come in with a shortness of breath and cough have been diagnosed and treated for bronchial asthma at other hospitals.
What would be the problem here?
I was so puzzled and baffled that I was deeply troubled.

Ninety percent of the patients who come to the clinic with a cough that has lasted for more than two months have been diagnosed and treated for reflux esophagitis at other hospitals, with no improvement.
Patients with shortness of breath and cough almost always come to us because they have been diagnosed with bronchial asthma and have not improved with treatment. After considerable thought, I found the answer.
A simple chest radiograph is taken by the doctor who sees the patient for a cough or shortness of breath lasting more than two months. Every doctor knows that a simple chest radiograph should be taken when a cough or shortness of breath is present for more than two weeks.
The Korea Disease Control and Prevention Agency and the Ministry of Health and Welfare even launched a campaign that aired during primetime television news to remind people to get chest radiography for coughs lasting longer than two weeks. In a country where tuberculosis is common, the idea of getting simple chest radiography for coughs lasting longer than two weeks is an excellent idea.
The problem is that few respiratory diseases can be detected by simple chest radiography. Furthermore, even advanced lung cancer may appear normal on a simple chest radiograph.
The experience of COVID-19 has also raised awareness among doctors and the public about the need to take chest radiography for coughing or shortness of breath. In the past, a few patients refused when asked

to take a simple chest photograph. These days, patients rarely say no to simple chest radiography when recommended.

The 67-year-old female patient also said she had simple chest radiography at several hospitals in Busan. She said they had conducted pulmonary function tests. After seeing the patient, it was clear her condition was serious. When listening to her breathing, I could hear stridor from the trachea. The presence of stridor, a band of frequencies lower than a whistle, in the airway may indicate that the patient's condition is extremely critical.
In these cases, bronchoscopy should be performed even if simple chest radiography comes out normal. This could indicate a tumor or foreign body in the airway or an obstruction in the upper airway. A simple chest radiograph was also normal.
At our clinic, two specialists read the simple chest radiographs to improve the accuracy of the reading. One of the specialists is me, a pulmonologist. The other is a radiologist.
I am not paid extra for reading, but the radiologist is paid to do the reading. As a pulmonologist, I have seen millions of simple chest radiographs, and I am considered an expert.

Human mistakes can always occur. To increase the accuracy of the readings, a double safeguard is provided by a pulmonologist and a radiologist. This is a fantastic combination. The pulmonologist looks at the patient, knows the patient's current symptoms, and takes a reading. The radiologist does not know the patient's information and only sees the image to read it as is. There are pros and cons. A pulmonologist examines the patient and reads the photos with a suspicion of certain diseases. A radiologist sees and reads images as objects.
Therefore, a pulmonologist looks at an image from a subjective perspective, whereas a radiologist only looks at objective data. It is certainly a fantastic combination of subjective and objective perspectives. As the simple chest radiograph appeared normal, could I treat this patient for asthma as I would in any other hospital?
I have said that a good doctor is a doctor who has just one more

thought.

Even if a simple chest radiograph is normal, two more tests should be performed: a chest CT scan and bronchoscopy. If a chest CT scan comes back normal, bronchoscopy should be performed.

That is what a good doctor would do. A good doctor should be a master at knowing all the different things that can happen to a patient, knowing how to do tests to diagnose hidden diseases accurately and having the ability to perform those tests.

A chest CT scan reveals a tumor surrounding the patient's trachea. As the tumor grew around the trachea and compressed it, it caused the patient's airway to narrow, resulting in the stridor. Moreover, it was not just growing around the trachea. As the disease progressed, the tumor invaded the trachea and was spreading into it. The patient was in an urgent condition. Surgical treatment was not an option.

She needed a bronchoscopy as soon as possible to take samples of the tumor for biopsy and remove the part of the tumor that was blocking her trachea to help with breathing. A biopsy should be performed quickly to determine the exact cause of the tumor and choose the appropriate chemotherapy or radiation treatment.

If this patient had come to the clinic a bit later, she would have lost her life. She would have died in immense pain. Even at the clinic, if I had given her asthma medication without following my usual conviction to think about one more thing, the outcome would have been no different.

It does not take a good doctor to do this. This is what all doctors are supposed to do.

A good doctor does not neglect their duty. This attitude is probably not unique to doctors. Truth is never far away. The real truth is right around us and available if we put our minds to it.

Just one more thought for the patients could change their lives, could it not? Many patients have seen me; I have treated critical respiratory patients today, and I will be doing the same thing tomorrow.

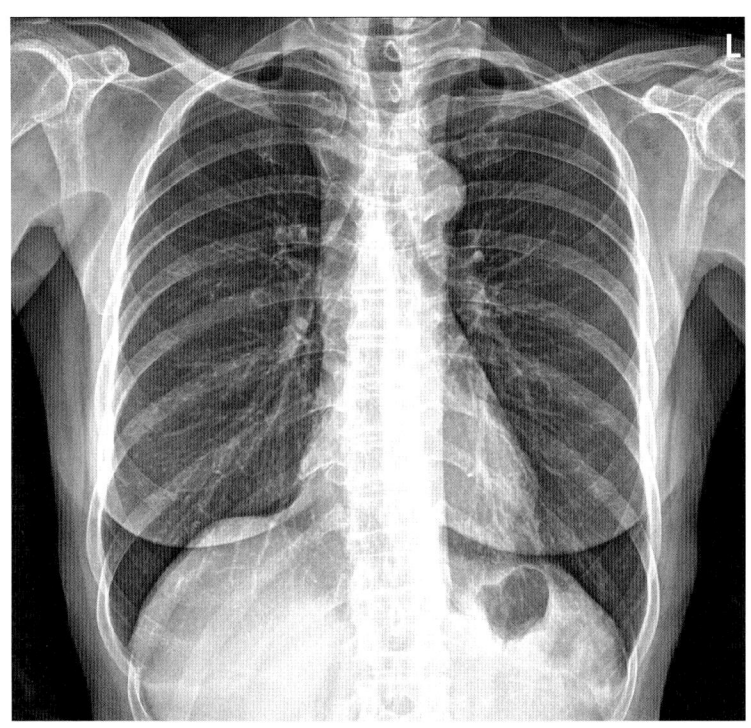

Simple chest radiograph of a 67-year-old female patient:
Normal chest with no abnormal findings.

	Name	
2024-06-07	ID	107566
REPORT	Age, Sex	067Y F
Beautiful Breath Clinic	Birth date	

Chest PA:

No active lesion.
Heart is not enlarged.
No evidence of pleural thickening.

Conclusion; Normal chest.

Radiologist

Official reading document from radiologist: Normal chest.

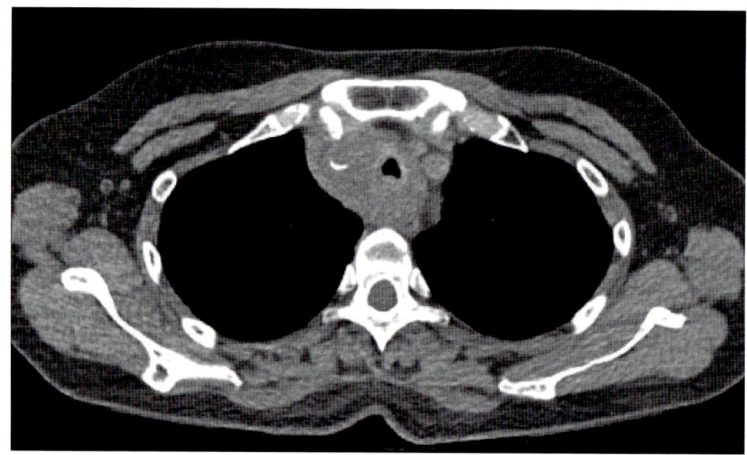

Narrowed trachea due to tumors surrounding it.

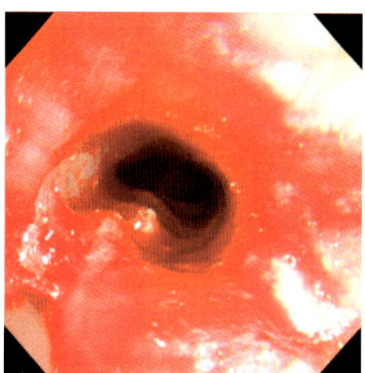 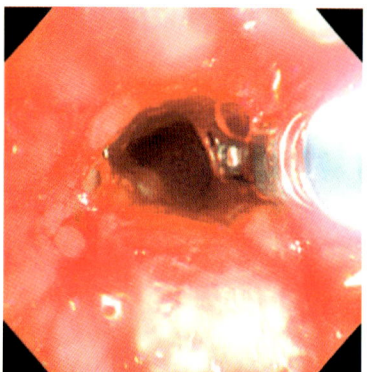

Bronchoscopic findings:
Tumor invading the trachea.

Bronchoscopy:
Photograph of a biopsy.

〚 Epilogue 〛

Remembering a day in 2018 when I thought I was living life to the fullest.

On April 27, 2018, I published "I 'Need' You Whenever I 'Breathe'." With considerable interest from general readers and patients alike, the book became the number 1 health essay in the medical community within a week of its release. I received many letters from patients and readers and encouragement and support from many patients I met in the clinic. I even received a long thank-you note from an expatriate. A lot has happened in those six years.

The biggest change was the COVID-19 outbreak, which started in China in late 2019. After the first confirmed case of COVID-19 in South Korea in January 2020, the virus began its frightening spread worldwide. Initially, many experts predicted the COVID-19 pandemic would be over in a period of six months to one year, which turned out to be false.

There has been a tremendous wave of change in our health and wellness and our economic and industrial structure. Working from home became a new normal, and people were legally restricted from gathering. Many healthcare workers have struggled. There have also been tragic losses of life. There was also a new type of depression called "corona blues."

My life as a pulmonologist has also changed. Our existing respiratory patients have suffered from respiratory sequelae from COVID-19 infection, and we have been careful to prevent infection in our staff when treating and caring for patients. A doctor I knew died within a week of being infected with COVID-19. It was a time of fear, suffering, and frustration.

Six years ago, I concluded the book "I 'Need' You Whenever I 'Breathe'" by sharing these words in the "Epilogue."

"This too shall pass" does not comfort those suffering from shortness of breath because the pain of shortness of breath is unbearable for even a moment.

Even six years ago, as a pulmonologist, I considered the suffering of those with shortness of breath, a problem of "breathing," to be the most painful among the symptoms of various respiratory diseases.

Since the COVID-19 pandemic, the Beautiful Breath Clinic has seen a significant increase in the number of patients with severe respiratory conditions coming to the clinic, with the proportion of visits from these patients exploding in 2023.

Moreover, the reduction of healthcare services at university hospitals and shrinkage of emergency departments began after the government's announcement in February 2024 that it would increase the number of medical students by 2,000 (radically increasing the number of medical students by 2,000 from 2025—an increase of 10,000 in five years), followed by the resignation of residents and the movement of compliance with the work schedule and resignation of professors. This situation has driven the critically ill patients to the Beautiful Breath Clinic.

The clinic was scheduled to open at 8 a.m., but patients would have been waiting since 6 a.m. Every day was a war.

This was also the time when the idea for this book, "I Am Dr. SEONGLIM JIN, a Pulmonologist," was conceived. The painful and sad stories of the patients I have seen and treated belong to the past.

Essential healthcare collapsed, followed by a surge in critically ill patients. The government, which was supposed to prevent the collapse of essential healthcare, made a misdiagnosis, and its insistence on that misdiagnosis led to an overprescription of the wrong remedies.

It is said that there is a hero in turbulent times, but a hero has been nowhere to be seen. I was frustrated. This is why I started writing again.

The past 30 years of my life as a pulmonologist have been harrowing yet dazzlingly brilliant. My day at the clinic was like a war, with anxiety and fear engulfing me, but it was also a happy day.

The pain of seeing my patients suffer made me sad, and the joy of seeing them recover made me happy.

I was always at the intersection of opposite emotions and sentiments.

A sentiment is different from an emotion. A sentiment is the quality of sensing a stimulus or change in a stimulus and is a concept that corresponds to rationality, referring to the human cognitive ability to sense and recognize external objects with the five senses and form representations.

An emotion, however, is a state of mind or feeling in response to a phenomenon or event. I came to see life through the lens of my perceptual abilities, forming my representation of respiratory patients' pain and suffering. I grew weary of the successes and failures of the treatments I encountered in my work as a doctor.

A sense of pressure kicks in as soon as I open my eyes at dawn. Physical fatigue and burnout are waiting for me at the end of a long day of practice.

Where will this road end?

My heart, praying with my hands clasped together in supplication, is not like that of a monk seeking the truth. I hope for peace for the many patients I have seen in my 30 years as a doctor and the happiness of their families.

My greater desire is for my peace of mind and relief from my physical fatigue. I hope that essential healthcare in South Korea will be reorganized so that patients can feel safe and healthy. How much time do I have left to serve my role in essential healthcare?

I hope to see a society where young doctors, who are the new future leaders, can work in a medical environment where they feel a sense of pride, mission, and respect.

I would like to express my heartfelt and sincere gratitude to the patients who inspired me and gave me the courage to write this book, entitled "I Am Dr. SEONGLIM JIN, a Pulmonologist." I dedicate this work on my life as a pulmonologist to my beloved mother and family, who have always been by my side, and my father, who is now at peace in Heaven.

> Above all else, guard your heart,
> for everything you do flows from it.
>
> - Proverbs 4:23

A pleasant conversation with the staff on a day in April 2024
at the Beautiful Breath Clinic.